The Abbot of Morpheus: First Epoch

Gerfarer

Published by Gerfarer, 2024.

While every precaution has been taken in the preparation of this book, the publisher assumes no responsibility for errors or omissions, or for damages resulting from the use of the information contained herein.

THE ABBOT OF MORPHEUS: FIRST EPOCH

First edition. October 21, 2024.

Copyright © 2024 Gerfarer.

ISBN: 979-8227181541

Written by Gerfarer.

Foreword

The Abbot of Morpheus is an interesting and provocative conversation between an Abbot and a Seeker. The Seeker's quest to find meaning in life leads him to meet the Abbot of Morpheus in a dream world called Morpheus. The conversation delves into many various aspects of life and the human condition. It explores themes like truth, love, God and the Divine, religion and dogmas, soul and eternity, Existence, belief and believing, free will, desire, choice, good and evil.

It also touches on the Devil, Oneness and separation, equality of people, cooperation and unity, purpose and meaning of life, Heaven and Hell, Judgement, faith, afterlife, birth and death, slavery, society and culture, poverty, intelligence, and intellect, alien life, and superintelligence, ego, or false self, etc. The author, cohesively, discusses the meaning, correlation, and cause-effect of the themes amply enough to be understood.

It offers its readers a spellbinding experience; stoking questions of great concern for everyone. It is written in prose poetry and takes the format of a long colloquy between the Seeker and the Abbot of Morpheus. The conversation takes place in a hypothetical place in the Seeker's dream called the inner court of Morpheus and is meant to answer his questions about his life on Earth from the perspective of the Abbot of Morpheus.

The author had settled on the use of a dreamscape as a setting for the conversation because he wanted to underscore the message that is being communicated in the book. A journey inward into the human psyche to understand oneself is desperately needed in the world which is sorely divided along many contentious lines. The dreamscape as used in this book can be seen as a metaphor for a deeper state of consciousness where it is possible to come into direct knowledge of what the human being is through observation and self-inquiry. It encourages conscientious and curious people to self-inquiry to understand themselves and their equality with the rest of the world and express the same in love and unity.

The Abbot of Morpheus seeks to demystify spirituality and to promote self-inquiry, equality of humanity, love, and unity towards a future of intelligent self-realized people living for the progress of the world. It underscores division at the very root of the individual, as the primary source of conflict between people, religions, nations, and indeed races. The book is the culmination of many years of the author's self-inquiry and contemplation on extensive material on a wide range of spiritual topics and life.

But **who is Gerfarer?** Gerfarer is the pen name of the author. He is a middle-aged male, who lives at the intersection of certain coordinates on the globe. He drinks tea with a few squeezes of lemon and three sugars in the morning and listens to podcasts before going to sleep in the night. He breaks down everything and then helps you to rebuild it back together and encourages you to discern for yourself. Gerfarer offers a fresh line of questioning and answering which would be interesting to curious people who are seeking liberation.

The Conversation

Abbot: "Who knocks, is that you, my son? Come in."

Seeker: "Old sir, do you know me?"

Abbot: "Yes, I know your heart, my son."

Seeker: "Please tell me who you are and where we are?"

Abbot: "I am the Abbot of Morpheus, and we are in Morpheus, the world of dreams."

Seeker: "Am I dreaming?"

Abbot: "Yes, son. Your quest for wisdom has led you in your dream to Morpheus. And your arrival into the inner court of Morpheus has granted you with the ability to recollect your earthly identity and memory so that you might ask any questions you have about your life on Earth."

Seeker: "So, this is all not real?"

Abbot: "It is real my son. You are here, aren't you? I am here, aren't I?"

Seeker: "Why do you call me son?"

Abbot: "Your arrival here is your birth into the inner court of Morpheus and all who arrive here are our sons."

Seeker: "What about women? Are they your daughters?"

Abbot: "All are sons; all are Adam. This door is shut to all earthly categories and castes. Only souls arrive here and they are our sons."

Seeker: "How shall I call you, old sir?"

Abbot: "I am the Abbot of Morpheus, but you can call me father."

Seeker: "Tell me one simple truth about everything I know as a man."

Abbot: "Son, man knows nothing. He is like a water molecule from a great river who suddenly thinks and tries to trace its existence from within the great river."

Seeker: "But isn't it possible for him to come to know this?"

Abbot: "From within the expanse of a single river? How presumptuous men can be, son."

Seeker: "Are there other rivers?"

Abbot: "Yes, my son. Innumerable they are; all headed to the coast of the Great Circle. Son, harken to my words; the Sun and the planets, the galaxies, and the universe, of both material and nonmaterial, all are bound together in a Great Circle, the consort of Existence. Like a water molecule of a river, like a whiff of vapor of an ocean, like a particle of a cloud, like a teeny-weeny snowflake, and like a drop of rain, man, and All, goes round and round the Great Circle; changing and unchanging, singing and dancing, doing, and resting, speaking, and listening, for eternity.

It is not just the river but what binds it and moves it; it is not just the vapor but what melts the water and raises it; it is not just the clouds but what condenses the vapor, holds it afloat in the sky, and breaks it into the water; it is not just the rain or snow but what causes them to fall, gather and stream. The Great Circle sees to it all; visibly and invisibly, in light and darkness, now and then, always, and forever.

It is everywhere and everything. It is in your eyes and looks out at everything, at itself; it is in the air you breathe and it is in your lungs; it is in the water you drink, and it is in your bladder; it is in the bread you eat, and it is in your stomach; it is in the ant, and it is in the whale; it is in the cosmos, far and near, big and small; it is the blue of the skies and oceans; it is in the silence of the dead of night, and it is in the sounds of the calm of a forest; it is in the love you give, and it is in the love you receive.

It is not everywhere nor in everything. It is not in a name nor a language; It is not in a wicked heart nor its deeds; it is not in a poisoned mind nor its products; it is not in thieving hands nor in the things they steal.

What would you like to know, son?"

Seeker: "Old sir, every other night when I go to sleep, I again find myself in a different dream world. Unknown to myself, I go about living from moment to moment; only to wake up to realize the fleetingness of what had been thought to be real life. I have witnessed mundane activities, earth-wobbling cataclysms, and sky-covered murals in my dreams, or Morpheus as you call it.

Just now, I was laid in bed, seeking to fall copiously asleep after juggling with the burdens of life. I thought of my day and some of the issues that confront me and the people I know. I was joyous that a day had been successful albeit its vicissitudes. Just now I was falling slowly into the mystery of sleep, how so that we are here."

Abbot: "A mystery has no explanation my son, that's why it's called a mystery."

Seeker: "But tell me, sir, are we there or here?"

Abbot: "We are always here my son, never there. Once a seeker knocks, we open the door and let them in, into a mystery beyond words my son. We never beckon anyone; they knock, and we let them in."

Seeker: "Father, many a night I have fallen into the arms of Morpheus and roamed her streets, met others, and enjoyed her fields and fruits. Why have I come across your door this night?"

Abbot: "Yes, indeed my son, and we have watched you come and go. Why only this night did you knock on our door? Every night across the Earth domain, billions of souls traverse these streets of Morpheus. Billions, my son but only a handful ever make their way to find our door and dare to knock. Millions of souls, my son, have knocked but only a spoonful is heard. Yet still thousands are heard but only a hundred persist. And even still my son, those who persist, desist when their faiths dwindle and are heard of no more. How sad to find and knock and be heard and yet desist. Here in our blissful repose, we wait for our sons but only half a dozen or so arrive every so often. We are glad for them and for the Great Circle."

Seeker: "How do dreamers find their way to your door, father?"

Abbot: "You dream according to your heart's contents and desires; according to what your soul yearns for the most. If it is truth and love, you shall find our door, son."

Seeker: "Will I have to knock tomorrow?"

Abbot: "Son, there is no tomorrow. You knock and arrive once. Once here, you're always here my son. Your tomorrow is also here; we never leave or retire, but always here round and round the Great Circle; enjoying blissfully and keeping the company of our sons."

Seeker: "Will I wake from Morpheus and return to the land of my birth?"

Abbot: "Yes but once arrived, always here. Here is not a place or land my son. You can always come and go from Morpheus but once accepted into the inner court of Morpheus, you're always here, and we're always here; for one cannot abandon his home. As for the land of your birth, what if I told you that you were never born?"

Seeker: "How so?"

Abbot: "Bodies are born and die, but no soul is ever born or dies. That which is eternal just is. Existence just is. The Great Circle just is. Man too, just is. Attempting to source its origin is but a fool's errand. We are all bound together for eternity. And through infinite earths and epochs, we traverse round and round the Great Circle forever. Yes, forever my son."

Seeker: "Please tell me more about my not being born."

Abbot: "The mystery of your earthly birth is but a regeneration into a new epoch. The mystery of your earthly life is but a playground of forms and their material expressions. A lofty play indeed but soon men grow weary and seek home. How sad that only a speck dares to knock hard enough to be heard. Ah, how sad. There was a song among the people of one of the earliest epochs that we still remember and love. It goes like this:

Nobody came to Earth to do a thing. Oh, Sons of Adam!

Here is our playground, both you male and female. Oh, Sons of Adam!

If one claims to be powerful, let them defeat death. Oh, Sons of Adam!

But if they cannot, let them love. Oh, Sons of Adam!"

Seeker: "Is it not enough that they are heard? Must they persist to knock until pitied?"

Abbot: "Who of you on Earth wakes upon the first cry of a rooster? And when you finally rise from your slumber, is the rooster pitied? Only the weightlessness of your heart, only the softness of your eyes, only the openness of your mind, and indeed my son, only your love opens the door. We barely touch the door handle. Ah, the weightlessness of your heart, my son."

Seeker: "What about deeds and actions? The temples and shrines we have built? The priests and scriptures of our prophets? The laws and authorities of our sects? Shall none of these lead a Seeker to arrive at your door?"

Abbot: "There is only one deed, and it is love which springs forth from the weightlessness of your heart. There is only one temple, and it is also in you, it is here. There is only one prophet and one word, and you are he. There are no laws except your volition, and there is no authority except that which springs forth from the weightlessness of your heart. Ah, the weightlessness of your heart my son."

Seeker: "Please father, can you unpack these mind-bending things you have just unleashed? If there is only one deed which is love, why does man hanker after so much?"

Abbot: "Son, man hankers after vanity which he knows not. Allowing his un-chaste mind to lead him in conflicting directions and deeds. Is compassion, not love? Is kindness, not love? Is faith, not love? Is joy, not love? Is neighborliness, not love? Is understanding, not love? Is forgiveness, not love? Is responsibility, not love? Is care, not love? Is making a promise, not love? Is trust, not love? Is respect, not love? Is patience, not love? Is anything beautiful, not love? Only one deed, son, and it is love. Truly, son, love conquers all they say. Is hate love? Is greed love? Is envy or jealousy love? Is backbiting love? Is lust love? Is pleasure love? Is separation love? Is sectionalism love? Indeed, son, is anything ugly love? There is no deed but love."

Seeker: "I am speechless."

Abbot: "Is silence not love?"

Seeker: "Indeed father. Ancient temples and shrines are dotted in many places on Earth. Our holy places; sacred and infallible, serve as points of contact with the Divine. These are reverent and pilgrimages are made to them. Why have you destroyed all these with just a few words? How so that you tell me there is only one temple which is in me, and it is here?"

Abbot: "Holy places you say, son? Who of you on Earth, dead or alive should exercise the right to designate a portion of Earth as holy, implying the rest unholy? Which builder or prophet can erect a building capable of containing the Magnificence of the Divine? What piece of location on Earth can be the home of the Divine? Can man not see that even the great Earth on which he lives is but a little piece of rock amid infinity? There is only one holy place my son. Only one and it is in you; we are here."

Seeker: "I am speechless"

Abbot: "Is silence not holiness?"

Seeker: "Indeed father. But man must embark on pilgrimages as the law demands. And when we go to these sites of holiness; rituals must be carried out in fine detail. We must wash and cleanse our bodies which are corrupted by our sinful lives, kiss walls, prostrate, jump, dance, throw stones and sticks at the Devil, and do all manner of rituals to the satisfaction of the Divine. It is written, it must be so. Perhaps you, the fathers here do not recognize Divine laws cast in gold and diamond, written on clay tablets and scrolls of thousands of years old and of unquestionable infallibility. Perhaps you're remiss in this father, surely?"

Abbot: "Harken to my words oh son and stop repeating the ignorance of Earthlings. There is only one pilgrimage and only one holy place. Why do you travel such long distances to find the Divine? The only pilgrimage requires no distance, it is always here; in the hallowed chambers of the weightlessness of your heart, in the glorious holy spirit that guides your mind, and inside every cell that regenerates your holy body. The Divine is not there, it is here, in you, my son. Do you imagine yourself too little to contain the

Magnificence of the Divine? Do you trivialize yourself so much that you prostrate to stars? Do you value language so much that you trust in written words? From our blissful repose, we have seen innumerable epochs come and go, each with their songs and words. Each with their prophets and priests, each with their sacredness, and alas, each with their illusions and delusions. Innumerable epochs, my son, but only one holiness which is in you."

Seeker: "Father, please go on. I am elated by your words."

Abbot: "Man has eyes that look outward and has an eye that looks inward. Surely, he who looks outwardly externalizes; scattering himself into tiny pieces and is subsumed by the intricate maze of materiality, he goes on seeking things, places, and prophets out there. Surely, he who looks inwardly gazes into the sublimity of holiness and is subsumed by the abyss of the Divine. Ah, the beauty of inward-looking."

Seeker: "Tell me more about my outward-looking father so that when I wake from Morpheus, I shall look well."

Abbot: "He who seeks outwardly moves from the holiness of silence into noise. He who seeks in the noise seeks to follow, he who seeks to follow shall be led, he who is led knows not himself, he who knows not himself shall be deceived and so the Earth has become a playground of grand deception, my son."

Seeker: "Father, who is behind this grand deception? The Devil? The Leader of the led? The Follower being led?"

Abbot: "Son, we here do not entertain the word Devil. Devil in your imperfect earthly language is the opposite of the Divine; a competitor of the Divine. Such faulty thinking does not spring forth from the wisdom of the spirit of mind but from man's ignorant fears. And both the leader and the led are equally deceived, my son. What causes the grand deception is not in any of these but rather in looking outwardly; a movement away from silence into words, deeds, things, places, and time. See to it that when you look outwardly, you do not stumble; that's all the use of man's outward-looking eyes."

Seeker: "But surely father, being led would guide a seeker from stumbling. Just like the blind needing to be walked."

Abbot: "Indeed son. The blind, having no use of their outward-looking eyes should be walked to avoid stumbling. To seek is not the same as walking on land and finding one's bearing; to seek is to remove the barrier of noise that separates the seeker from the Divine, who is already one with man. You cannot be led to that which you already are. To seek to be led is to reveal the ignorance of the seeker; which ignorance is imposed by the tapestry of the grand deception. Ah, the pains of deception and separation my son."

Seeker: "Please father, can you tell me more about being one with the Divine and how is it that It cannot be led to?"

Abbot: "Son, being led is not about navigating a landscape as I have already told you. Subjecting the spirit of mind to the instruction and direction of another is the pain of being led, my son. Can anything outside a circle discern anything inside the circle? And what makes a circle if not its completeness? For a circle that is even a fraction of a degree less would not be called a circle. And what can designate the beginning or ending point of a circle? So, like the Great Circle, man too is a circle; complete and eternal. He needs nothing outside his circle and nothing outside his circle is needed by him. He needs no cultures, no words, no rituals, no temples of stone or gold, no scriptures or books, no guidance, no prophets, no priests, no angels, no gods, and indeed, no outsiders.

He is complete and eternal. Ah, the beauty of completeness and eternity my son."

Seeker: "Father, it is also written that man is but an infant and sinful. That only through prophets and guidance can he be redeemed, that he must be cultured and beat into submission to become a righteous soul. Are all souls already complete?"

Abbot: "Yes, man is a destination; not a journey my son. He needs no rules nor rituals to become anything; he already is that which he is. He does not become but always is and will always be. Through infinite earths and epochs, he remains so; complete, wholesome, and eternal; born so and dies so. We have heard men say to one another, 'let us bind ourselves to this or that set of rituals, systems, and practices; so that we will become better souls in our next lifetimes'. We have also heard men say to one another, 'come you all let us follow this prophet and be a sect, for heaven awaits us if we are good souls and damnation awaits shoddy souls.' Does he consider himself incomplete and shoddy? That the Great Circle would churn such misery? His ignorant deeds or sins are but the fallout of the grand deception. Ah, the pains of ignorance my son."

Seeker: "What about submission to our gods? Who will answer our prayers if you say man needs no gods? Who will send down the rain? Who will fertilize the soil for our crops? Whose angels shall guard us and whisper their guidance into the ears of man? Who will save our souls from damnation in the afterlife?"

Abbot: "Man is already enveloped in absolute submission to the Great Circle my son. He eats from its bowl and drinks from its cup. His submission to that which he calls God is not a matter of choice; it is ordained in his heart. Against the wrangling of his promiscuous mind, his heart soaks in submission to the Great Circle; he cannot help it. He is in submission when he rises in the morning from Morpheus and he is in submission when he retires into Morpheus. He is in submission when he loves and when faithful. He is in submission both in defiance and obeisance. Your gods, from epoch to epoch are but a reflection of your divided nations and cultures.

As man appropriates the Divine for their cultures, the Great Circle rolls on in gigantic laughter. When you speak of gods, my son, see to it that you speak only of one Divinity and indeed, one Great Circle; even as you call it what you may. The Divine sees to the needs of man, adequately and abundantly, and Providence knocks on his door serendipitously without his needing to ask, or to beg, or to wish.

Man needs nothing outside his circle my son; not even your so-called angels. Do you imagine a gap between you and the one God? That He needs angels and messengers to speak to you? Step out of the bandwagon of self-deception and darkness into light and you will see too that man needs nothing outside his circle."

Seeker: "Father, a man is born into a family and a society; which have customs and traditions to culture him. Can he truly live outside his culture and still be wholesome and delightful in the Divine? These customs and traditions guide man from his evil ways and teach him the ways of his ancestors who had lived peaceably with the Divine and had been instructed to follow these self-same customs. These are passed on from generation to generation for the benefit of mankind. And we uphold and follow these customs and traditions to the glory of the Divine. How can I leave Morpheus convinced by you, Father, that all these are not needed by us?"

Abbot: "We here do not have any interest in convincing our sons. We only blow away the mist and dust of illusions so that you may see well. From the first man to your millions and billions and from epoch to epoch, we see you grow your languages and societies; we see you invent your laws and customs; we see you gleefully and painfully bind yourselves to the traditions and rituals of your forebears; we see you divide yourselves into castes, tribes, and nations; we see you hold on to your divisions and pains like a hungry ferocious dog to a bone.

We see you assert your divisions over the colors of your bodies and eyes; we see you erect great walls between your lands; we see your divisions bring you wars and violence with untold calamities; we see your wars wreak havoc across the Earth domain; we see you gut each other down like weeds and we see all the greed and insidiousness of your divisions. My son, we have seen all this from our blissful repose and we have equally seen the pains and miseries that lay within them. Is division not the very essence of your cultures?"

Seeker: "Indeed father. Should our divisions cease?"

Abbot: "Should your pains continue?"

Seeker: "Indeed not father. Can you please tell me more about our divisions? Are we not divided because we are different by nature? There are nations and cultures whose descendants are wealthy because the Divine has blessed them more and chosen them to rule the Earth. And alas father, there are the great majority of people whose very appearance speaks volumes of Divine neglect. And yes, Father, mankind is also divided by the colors of their bodies and eyes. There are whole tribes of midgets and pygmies who would certainly not agree with you that nature has created us equal. There are whole nations who have known nothing but slavery and poverty from time immemorial, surely, they would not nod in agreement too."

Abbot: "My son, that which makes you equal is not in your physical appearances as men; that which makes you equal is not in your stature or color of your bodies and eyes, nor is it in the gametes you carry. That which makes you equal is not in your wealth; that which makes you equal is not in your social status. That which makes you equal is certainly not in your cultural advancement nor is it in the divinity of your forebears. That which makes you equal as men is not in any of these factors of your divisions but rather, son, that which makes men equal is the undying soul substance in them. Only that which is permanent is the joy and substance of your equality and eternity.

Your physical body dies; so, it is not permanent. Your wealth withers; so, it is not permanent. Your titles and accolades are meaningless in the longevity of time. Your cultures and the achievements of your forebears are subject to the inevitable death of your epoch; then rises another epoch with its vicissitudes, round and round the Great Circle my son. That which makes you equal is undying and permanent.

The beauty of nature is in its variety. If the rainbow was made of the same color, would it still be pleasing to look at? Roses alone do not make a beautiful garden; so, a good gardener would mix plants and flowers of different colors and fragrances. Don't fault nature for your differences, look to your selves and how you have allowed yourselves to be drawn away from your inner sanctuary into the noise of deception."

Seeker: "Father, please tell me more about the physical differences and similarities among men?"

Abbot: "Son, do all men have legs, feet, arms, and hands? And do these perform the same tasks though the men themselves may be of different social classes, races, and cultures?"

Seeker: "Yes, Father; all men have legs, feet, arms, and hands and they indeed perform the same tasks. Legs and feet are for walking and arms and hands are for working."

Abbot: "Is that not equality? Again son, do all men have instruments for sensing their environment? That is, do all men have eyes, ears, noses, tongues, and skins though the men themselves may be of different social classes, races, and cultures?"

Seeker: "Yes, father; they do indeed. All men have eyes for looking at the beautiful landscapes of nature; ears for hearing the caws of crows; noses for smelling the sweet fragrance of frankincense; tongues for tasting the saltiness of a dish; and skins for feeling the soothing breezes of a beach, father."

Abbot: "Is that not equality? Again son, do all men have brains though the men themselves may be of different social classes, races, and cultures?"

Seeker: "Yes, father; they do indeed. All men have brains, and they function with the same processes and substances; throughout the nervous system."

Abbot: "Is that not equality? And, do these brains operate based on the data and education their cultures provide; so that a farmer is adept at crops because his culture is peasantry and a philosopher is so because his culture has an academy?"

Seeker: "Indeed Father, it is as you say; underlying the differences is the same brain."

Abbot: "Correct, son. The differences are cosmetic and inconsequential."

Seeker: "Father, you said what makes men equal is the soul. What about their physical equality?"

Abbot: "Son, what moves the limbs? What sees the beautiful landscapes? What hears the caws? What tastes the saltiness? What feels the breeze? What ignites the brain? What makes the body tick?"

Seeker: "The soul."

Abbot: "Correct, son. The body is a vehicle for the soul. Dwell in your equality."

Seeker: "I am humbled by your words, father. Should we embrace our differences?"

Abbot: "Yes, son. But deny your divisions."

Seeker: "Can ordinary men bring our divisions to an end? For everywhere there's division, there's the unassailable might of the wealthy and powerful, who delight themselves very much in our divisions."

Abbot: "Indeed, son. Ah, the pains of ignorance."

Seeker: "Are the wealthy and powerful also ignorant? How so and why have they come to be masters of the Earth domain, father?"

Abbot: "Son, ignorance of self leads men to seek wealth and power; while fueling your divisions. Self-knowledge obliterates ignorance and vanity; leading men to seek unity and humanity. Can men be united where the prize is profit, whether wealth or power?"

Seeker: "Indeed not, father. But is this not because man is by nature ambitious and greedy?"

Abbot: "Son, man's ambitions must spring forth from the weightlessness of his heart. It is the love man has for growth and flourishing. Can there be true growth where man's ambitions are tied to his personality, a mere garment? As I have already told you, a man's body dies, so, it is not permanent. His titles and so-called legacies are weightless in the winds of time and like chaff, float off to oblivion sooner or later. Were he wiser than he pretends to be, his ambitions would be tied to the collective good and unity of the world. Ah, the pains of ignorance my son."

Seeker: "And his greed?"

Abbot: "Would he be greedy if his ambition is tied to the collective good and unity of the world?"

Seeker: "Indeed not. But father, mankind has built a world that exalts these qualities; where wealth, power, and fame underlie prestige and social status. These in turn bring to people the love and respect of their fellow men. And father, it is not just these abstract qualities of love and respect but also, all the good and pleasurable things of life are easily attainable by wealth and power. What is the world and living if one cannot enjoy its blessings and beauties? Are the happiness and sweetness that fill the belly and chest when others bow in respect and admiration utter vanity? The limitless expansion one feels when their fame goes before them and to every nook and cranny of the Earth is certainly covetous, wouldn't you say, father?"

Abbot: "Yes, indeed son. All these are coveted by man. But is man's covetousness tied to the collective good and unity of the world? Wealth and fame are not evil per se, nor utterly vain. They become vain and the source of evil when they are coveted for one-upmanship either for the individual or the group over humanity. Son, when men talk of power, it is laughable. To enjoy the subjugation of and prostration from other men is truly the highest point of being lost amid deception and is also a fanfare for ignorant fools. For that which deserves your subservience and prostration is beyond the realm of the Earth domain. And for one body to bow to another body, both of which die, is moot in the grand scheme of the Great Circle.

Remember son, the Great Circle keeps rolling and rolling, that which changes or dies cannot be important. Only that which is permanent is the joy of your equality and eternity. One soul must not bow or prostrate to another and the other soul must not allow this. In the end, vanity is suspended from ignorance. Ah, the pains of ignorance my son."

Seeker: "Father, I see what you're saying to be the truth; that which is. But my mind is wrestling with the realities on Earth. Billions of people are lined up in fellowship of sectarian dogmas; emanating from our ancient past of thousands of years ago. These dogmas have in turn produced massive institutions that confer great titles on their adherents. These gargantuan figures claim to act at the behest of the Divine and therefore proffer to mankind its guidance and direction. Can all these truly be suspended from ignorance, or is it something else?"

Abbot: "Where there is personal gain or profit; where men seek power; where status and prestige are present; sadly, truth becomes a casualty. And when truth becomes a casualty, dogmas and theories spring up like mushrooms. Son, unburden your heart and mind with external squabbles of men and let your love guide and direct your steps and works of your hands to the glory of the Divine. Did you not understand when I said man is complete, wholesome, and eternal? And that he needs nothing outside his circle and nothing outside his circle is needed by him? Are dogmas not part of the building blocks of your cultures? And is division not the very essence of your culture? Harken to my words oh son."

Seeker: "Thank you for reminding me, Father. What about men who become enlightened, evolved, and elevated to the high offices of the Divine? That is, those who claim to wine and dine with the Divine Deity and create a cult following to impart His messages and instructions to their flock. These have been called powerful men of God and indeed Father, they exercise immense power over their fellow men and proffer all manner of systems and rituals; to as it were, lead their flock to the threshold of the Divine. What is the nature of the link between man and the one God?"

Abbot: "Son, call it what you may; Divine Deity, the one God, the Most-High, the Supreme God and all the other appellations man has placed on it since time immemorial, the Great Circle is in man and man is in It. When you talk of a link between man and the one God, you're suggesting that two separate entities are being connected by some medium, is that not so?"

Seeker: "Yes father. And this medium, could it be composed of special men or angels or prophets or other god-whisperers?"

Abbot: "Son, this is a great fallacy upon which the grand deception subsists. Once you're sold on a medium then intercessors spring up from nowhere; and authorities and dogmas are formed, albeit speculatively. There's no medium between man and his maker, for they are one. And with infinite eyes and ears, the Great Circle sees and hears all there is to see and hear. And with infinite legs and hands, the Great Circle walks and works all there is to walk and work on. And with infinite wings and fins, the Great Circle flies and swims all there is to fly and swim. And with infinite hearts and souls, the Great Circle feels and spreads Its love across existence. Remember son, there's no medium, only Oneness."

Seeker: "But why is this not obvious to man? Why is he eager to be led, to be taught, to be enjoined, and to supplicate for favors, Father?"

Abbot: "Ah, the wonders of ignorance my son."

Seeker: "What about fear? What role does fear play in leading man to seek outwardly, father?"

Abbot: "Fear in grown men is like what a scarecrow is to children. Is a scarecrow, not a hoax? Sadly, son, most men have still not lost their baby teeth and as such cannot chew meat. They prefer to suckle milk from the breasts of whisperers. Pretending to be children helps them avoid facing what they are; while insisting on being infantile calms them to hold onto their illusions; and embracing their fears, they become vulnerable to mediums, and charlatans.

Son, if you must know, then know this; fear is a needless flight away from the silence of the soul, away from the timeless and endless gaping void, and alas, away from the centerless soul of man."

Seeker: "I am flabbergasted, father. What would cause us to be mature grown people? What will lead us to be self-sufficient? What would extinguish fear of self?"

Abbot: "Self-knowledge. Self-understanding. Self-love. For if you do not know yourself by yourself for yourself, you cannot understand what you are, and without understanding what you are, how can you love yourself? Without loving yourself, the serenity of thc soul becomes disturbed and fear takes root.

To remove fear and squalor from the inner sanctuary, man must look inwardly and embrace his Oneness with the Divine, son."

Seeker: "Father, could you please elaborate on Oneness with the Divine?"

Abbot: "When man retreats from all that which is not him; what is left is the silence of Oneness."

Seeker: "What is left, father?"

Abbot: "Your question, son, suggests that you're seeking to be told, to be led, and to be deceived. Only man can negate all that which is not himself, and only he may find that which remains."

Seeker: "Indeed, father. Help me then."

Abbot: "Again son, only man can help himself."

Seeker: "Indulge me, father."

Abbot: "Retreat inwardly and negate all that which is not you, son. Don't strain, don't exert effort; be still and let it come to you. See your body dismember into a billion pieces and drop off to the Earth; see your thoughts wiggle up and down and quiet down like a resting well-fed puppy; sink into the abyss of nothingness and be caught and cushioned by the buoyancy of the Divine. Reside there in Oneness and let your love uncover holy understanding."

Seeker: "Surely father, this will take some practice and time to master."

Abbot: "It takes no practice and time. You cannot practice awareness nor truth; it dawns on you from where you do not look and at a moment you are not searching for it. For that which observes and searches is that which is being observed and searched for. But when the searching stops and the observer effect is no longer active, then awareness and truth come seeping out of the nothingness of no-thought and no-self. Let the love of self lead the way, my son."

Seeker: "Self-love is a ubiquitous expression on the lips of man. Often people say they love themselves; is this what you mean by self-love?"

Abbot: "Do not pay mind to such casual statements and frivolousness. What they mean when they say that, is their egoistic mind projecting itself for public acceptance. Son, they are referring to the love of their ego-image; vanity galore. Self-love needs no verbal expression. It is deep, silent, and resides in your inner light."

Seeker: "But fear drives men away from looking inwardly."

Abbot: "No, son. Fear drives children away from looking inwardly. Ah, what a scarecrow man has become unto himself."

Seeker: "Father, what is the nature of the silence that makes men afraid when they look inwardly?"

Abbot: "Son, men approach the inner sanctuary from the center of their egoistic mind, and the ego, being what it is, is fearful and grandly limited. For a limited mind cannot hold within its confines, the limitless space and energy that emit from the centerless soul of man. Thus, when the egoistic mind is challenged to its summit of limitation and therefore unable to hold the vibrations of higher frequencies, fear becomes an automatic reaction; causing flight and descension from the higher realms to the egoistic mind and its familiar mundane objects and attachments. Ah, the limits and fears of the ego my son."

Seeker: "What silent thoughts or affirmations should we have when in silence?"

Abbot: "My son, do not confuse the absence of speech with the silence of the soul. For in this great silence, there's no mind to think and there's no one to affirm his meager desires. The ego and its shenanigans are obliterated. And the selfless soul substance comes afield from the timeless and endless gaping void. It is in that void that you may know yourself by yourself for yourself."

Seeker: "Father, what is knowing yourself by yourself for yourself?"

Abbot: "Son, you cannot know yourself from an external source as man is a circle; complete and impenetrable. So, when you look inward and come to know yourself, you cannot also communicate to others what you find. You may wish to but you'll not find the words; for language and words become utterly useless. You can know it but you cannot speak it; and when you speak, you tell a lie, even to yourself; for that which speaks is not that which knows.

The describer may describe but the description is not the actual thing being sought to be described. When you're seized by silence and collapsed by the timeless and endless gaping void; what use are words and what need is speech?"

Seeker: "What use is self-knowledge if it cannot be used to teach and help others, father?"

Abbot: "You cannot have a motive for self-knowledge, son. You cannot also teach self-knowledge to others nor can you help others to achieve it. You may point to the mountain to show others as an act of love but they would have to scale it to the top by themselves to know. You cannot climb to the mountaintop and capture what you see in words and share it with others for what you put into words may be inaccurate or misconstrued. The seeing is the knowing and the knowing cannot be communicated; nor can it be put to words in whatever way and shared with others. Symbols may do justice to it but cannot also be accurate, son."

Seeker: "Father, can self-knowledge and spiritual quest lead man to gain supernatural powers?"

Abbot: "Son, self-knowledge is not a sensationalist quest for personal aggrandizement of any sort. It would not make you fly; for you can build an airplane. It would not make you walk on water; for you can build a boat. It would not make you a magician; for you can build a circus. It would not make you travel back in time; for you can build a better future. Before a man speaks of gaining supernatural powers, has he known himself and gained his natural powers? Before man builds castles in the air, has he finished exploring the caves for hidden treasures? Son, self-knowledge is a serious endeavor of a journey home, back to the source of all powers; love."

Seeker: "But man is not an island unto himself. He is surrounded by friends and family; others who might benefit from a self-realized fellow."

Abbot: "Two self-realized fellows would benefit each other very much by merely sitting in silence. But one self-realized man cannot help the other who is not, even with all the words and all the languages of the world. It is not a thing to be told, it is to be known directly from within one's circle. Ah, the joy and beauty of man's circle my son."

Seeker: "Does the need to belong to a community; and to be prideful of one's culture and customs lead man to cast aside self-inquiry and seek outwardly?"

Abbot: "Yes, son, it is as you say. Out of naiveté and ignorance, man is sometimes overwhelmed by his community and culture, and sometimes the need to belong comes from man's fear of himself, which he knows not. Not knowing himself, he takes flight to conform; to feel assured. But alas, both his fear and the assurance of his community are a grand hoax. As for being prideful, my son, it is unfathomable for a precious thing as life to be wasted in foolishness and superficiality. Wouldn't you give up your culture and unfree yourself from its fetters; to taste the sweetness of knowing and owning yourself? Ah, the joy of knowing oneself, my son."

Seeker: "Can congregations be likened to herds? And father, why are the currents of congregations so strong? Currents that draw men, in their multitudes, outwardly; away from themselves and have stood strong for thousands of years. This is certainly a reality on Earth and has been accepted as the way it is. Is it possible for these currents to abate and give way for a community of self-knowing men?"

Abbot: "Son, have you not read in the history books of Earth about times past when empire builders invoked the name of the Divine for their ends? When man was whipped and forced into conformity? When the only chance man had to stay alive was to conform? When man was overwhelmed by the brutalities of zealous religious wars and persecutions? When congregations were formed out of the ashes of death and pain? After all these centuries of being whipped away from themselves into herds, they may have forgotten how it all happened and believe there's no other way. Man has been estranged from himself and the only familiar thing he knows is to conform to a herd. Yes, son, a better world is possible and inevitable when man realizes that one ought to know oneself by oneself for oneself. Ah, what a joyous future awaits man."

Seeker: "Are you saying, father, that congregational spirituality is a phase in the development of man toward a better future?"

Abbot: "Yes, son. From the caves to the stars, man will rise to ride the heavens."

Seeker: "You mean ride the heavens in the afterlife?"

Abbot: "No, son. I mean the effervescence of life will blossom and spread out into the cosmos. Man will not only gaze at stars, he'll ride the heavens. Harken to my words oh son."

Seeker: "Indeed, father. Also, I have read a great deal about man's past; am I being corrected now that the wars and persecutions that were waged in the name of God were far from being sanctioned by the one God?"

Abbot: "If God is one, and He is; if Heaven is one, and it is; if the Divine is one, and it is; if Creation is one, and it is and if indeed, all is Oneness; how can there be divisions and factions amongst the children of the world? How can the one God sanction such an abomination for His children?"

Seeker: "But the wars and persecutions are waged by the righteous against heathens and pagans who would not yield to God otherwise."

Abbot: "In whose judgment are the righteous acclaimed righteous? In whose judgment are the pagans condemned as pagans? Is it in the judgment of your dogmas, or sages, or prophets, or seers, or messengers, or redeemers? Is it in the judgment of those who see God in burning fires, see visions in their dreams, or hear angelic voices? Or is it in the judgment of empire and nation builders? Would man not proclaim and say what he must if it serves his cause and if there is profit in sight? Ah, the pains of self-serving whisperers my son."

Seeker: "Father, are there whisperers or mediums who are not self-serving?"

Abbot: "Where there is no personal gain or profit, where men do not seek power, and where status and prestige are not the motive; then truth may be exalted. And men being social creatures may share their love in words and kindness with one another.

And again son, where there are totalitarian claims; where men claim mediumship or authority, or where men claim to be representatives of the one God or working at His behest and the like, be rest assured that, they are lying to your faces. But be careful, for if you call them out, they may hang you; your history books should teach you better in this regard.

If you must know, son, then know this; violence is the weapon of truth-mufflers. So, he who knows does not speak; he resides in the boundless oceans of silence. Ah, the safety of silence my son."

Seeker: "Is silence better than martyrdom?"

Abbot: "Yes, son. A thousand songs may be sung for martyrs but if one were to share their love even for one more day with the world; it'd benefit the world more than a thousand songs. Words may be misconstrued, words may misinform and alas, words may be manipulated by truth-mufflers and killers of martyrs; but love is the only thing that penetrates the circle of man. Share your love, not words my son."

Seeker: "Father, it is my understanding that man's circle is impenetrable."

Abbot: "Yes, it is. Only love can penetrate it; for he and love are one, and like attracts like. Harken to my words oh son."

Seeker: "But a martyr's songs and example may inspire many, millions."

Abbot: "Yes, may or may not. Only love is certain to penetrate the core of man. Ah, the machinations of truth-mufflers my son, beware!"

Seeker: "Indeed, father. I am humbled by your wisdom. What is the nature of love?"

Abbot: "Son, to explain what love is will be an endless curly journey as we have already observed the fruitlessness of words. But since it is the only instrument we have, let me try. Love is man's light; a great beam of light with innumerable strands, that emits from the seat of man's essence. I can only name a few of these strands my son.

Intelligence is one of her strands and wisdom is the sister of intelligence. Perception is one of her strands and understanding is the sister of perception. Compassion is one of her strands and kindness is the sister of compassion. Passion is one of her strands and faith is the sister of passion. Action is one of her strands and ambition is the sister of action. Joy is one of her strands and happiness is the sister of joy. Integrity is one of her strands and honesty is the sister of integrity.

Son, I am beset by old age and cannot tell you more about the other strands of love. But the foregoing should provide you with some hints and encourage you to go on to peer into the beam of love yourself by yourself for yourself; for you are it."

Seeker: "Father, I am elated by your words; such fruitfulness. What is the nature of this light? Is it akin to the light of the Sun or the Moon?"

Abbot: "It is the light that beams out of your eyes when you rub sleep from your eyes, it is the light that illuminates Morpheus when you go to sleep, it is the light that glows your heart, it is the light of the spirit of mind, it is the light that circles in every cell of your body, it is the light others see when they look at you and you, them; it is you and you are it."

Seeker: "Strange words, father."

Abbot: "fret not son, they'll come to you. Do not strain for understanding because such a forced attempt will only bring you nothing. Brood in the inner sanctuary and cast aside the ego's feistiness; to bring the spirit of mind to a directionless stillness. It is there, that you'll find holy perception and understanding my son."

Seeker: "Thank you, father. But tell me, if man is love and from the foregoing, I see how powerful the light of love is, why does he not act his nature effortlessly? Why don't intelligence, compassion, and joy exude in his everyday life? Why is he so miserly with his nature? Why is self-pity killing his joy? Why has he replaced intelligence with folly and compassion with aggression? Why does his ambition lead him to greed and selfishness? Is man hopelessly estranged from himself?"

Abbot: "Estranged from himself? Yes. Hopelessly? No. He only needs to realize that he is going in the wrong direction and then turn inwardly. Once he does and is diligent, he'll soon see for himself the feistiness and veil of the ego. It is there and then that the death of the ego may be occasioned. And if so done, a new life will begin; one that is true to his nature. And who shall mourn for the death of the ego my son? Ah, what a joy to celebrate."

Seeker: "And what is the nature of this new life that begins after the death of the ego, father?

Abbot: "The ego dies but doesn't die; it recedes from the foreground and becomes diminutive in the human psyche, son. It is cut down to size and takes its place as a functional instrument in the life of the individual for his everyday life. As this happens, man is now centered in his true nature and he is intelligent, compassionate, sensitive, and more alive; energetic, and loving. His perception is wholesome and understanding flows to him. He is the originator of his knowledge and external sources become obsolete. His perception is sharp and sensitive; he could cut through a diamond to the very beginning of its formation.

The egoistic mind becomes naked and shies away into the background. His illusions die with his ego and the grand deception becomes a mere thing to diagnose. He unveils his own sage, prophet, and redeemer. He weds joy and happiness. Integrity and honesty underpin his every action, and ambition takes on its rightful cloak and diligence. In him is humanity defined and exemplified. Ah, what a joy to celebrate; the death of the ego my son."

Seeker: "Indeed father. But what is the ego?"

Abbot: "Son, man's true nature has been wholesome since time immemorial and cannot be adulterated. The ego is an invention of your culture and is installed in man's psyche through continuous benign and forced processes of conditioning which culminate in the ego personality and identity. The ego is a garment, a persona of sorts, required by your society and its chief instruments of operation are the intellect and memory. Man is born free of the ego but is cultured into one by the time he jettisons his innocence, my son."

Seeker: "Is the ego limited to mental activity?"

Abbot: "When the spirit of mind is forced aside and the egoistic mind reigns, then man's legs and hands walk and work his ego. His heart center is lost and his emotions are steered by his ego. His spleen and liver dance after his ego. He speaks what his ego wants to hear and hears what his ego wants to say. He becomes a play thing in the crafty feistiness of his ego. Ah, the crafty feistiness of the ego my son."

Seeker: "Please father, explain what you mean by the intellect and memory being the chief instruments of the ego."

Abbot: "Intelligence is incongruent with the ego and as such, the intellectual domain of man's psyche is employed by the ego. The intellect in turn operates on data to evaluate, estimate, measure, compare, judge, condemn, praise, and engage in all its feistiness. Memory is the storehouse of that data, son."

Secker: "What is intelligence?"

Abbot: "Son, to understand intelligence, you should first understand wisdom. Wisdom is the state or quality of the mind that man perceives through his intelligence. And a perception that is complete and wholesome is intelligent. Intelligence therefore is the use of the full complement of man's faculties all at once: integrity or the love of truth, memory, or records of that which has been, intellect or the instrument for mental navigation, clarity or the absence of distortions occasioned by the ego, imagination, or the capacity to see or think ahead of time and space, and other unknowable processes. The outcome or product of intelligence is the perception of what is or truth, either externally or internally.

Intelligence is a certain movement or vibration of the mind; it is still but dynamic, it is minuscule but gigantic, it is wholistic but multi-faceted and it is the same now and always."

Seeker: "Indeed, father. Is there something like superintelligence?"

Abbot: "No, son. Intelligence is the same everywhere and all time."

Seeker: "Is man today not more intelligent than he was during his cave days?"

Abbot: "No, son. Intelligence is of his soul and the soul is always complete, wholesome, and eternal. Man is as intelligent today as he was in the caves. He may have accumulated a lot of data or memory over the past millennia and he may have developed far more advanced measuring tools like space telescopes to gather more and more data, but the size of the data does not advance intelligence nor its fruit, truth. Truth is always the same and so is its perception my son."

Seeker: "Indeed, father. What about the possibility of alien life that may have superintelligence?"

Abbot: "Son, underlying the mechanics of intelligence is the love of truth. Truth is always what it is, whether on Earth, outside your solar system, or galaxy. Alien life may boast of more advanced measurements and data gathering, therefore more depth of perception but the mechanics of intelligence remain the same everywhere. They may equally boast of super technologies and technological products, they may know how to work with gravity or work with solar energy better than Earthlings, etc. but intelligent perception is the same. Intelligence is a gift of the Divine and all creation that have its capacity, enjoy it equally and abundantly. Man's intelligence is the self-same intelligence of his maker, and outside man and his maker, there's nothing that is unlike man or his maker."

Seeker: "Father, isn't it possible to find alien life that has better eyesight, hearing, or sensing that makes them more intelligent than man?"

Abbot: "Son, better eyesight, hearing, or sense do not have any bearing on intelligence. If someone can see ten kilometers ahead of another, it doesn't make them more intelligent. It may give them a deeper depth of understanding but that is a potential that the one with shorter eyesight may come to if they moved closer or developed a technology to also see ten kilometers ahead. A computer can multiply a set of numbers in a second and an abacus may take days but they would both arrive at the same result. What makes both the computer and the abacus the same in this case is not their speeds but rather, the use of the rules of multiplication. Similarly, the rules of perception are contained in intelligence. Do you follow, son?"

Seeker: "Yes, father. What about the intelligence of a child and that of a grown man?"

Abbot: "It is the self-same intelligence and perhaps even more pristine in the child which has not yet tainted its integrity with the ego. What the child lacks is data and not intelligence. A grown man may boast of many decades of experiences, learning all manner of things by trial and error or reading, etc. but all that is the accumulation of data and information. Therefore, having more data and information, he may be wiser and understand things better than the child could if he plies his perception with intelligence. But the mechanics of intelligence remain the same for both child and man because intelligence is of the soul and the soul is never a work in progress; it comes into life complete and wholesome and leaves life being the same. Ah, the eternity of the soul my son."

Seeker: "Father, what is the relationship between intelligence and intuition?"

Abbot: "Son, intuition is man's inner perception of knowledge which occurs to him without effort. Intuition could result from intelligence; in which case it serves man's quest for knowing and wisdom. But intuition could also result from man's egoistic mind and its endless groping for pleasure; in which case it is destructive. If man wants to be wise, let him quiet his egoistic mind to nurture and receive the silent beacons of his soul. But when a man is in his everyday life living from the strings of the ego, then intuition could precipitate from the background of his conditioning, his distorted memory, his false sense of reality, his deep-seated and perhaps even forgotten desires of the ego, etc. and intuition, therefore, loses its value of wisdom and festers the ego."

Seeker: "Father, are intuitions from intelligence messages from the spiritual realm to man to guide him?"

Abbot: "Intelligence is of the soul and the soul is man's bridge with the spiritual realm. The soul is Spirit and what Spirit says to man is wise indeed. Never has it been known for Spirit to misguide man but man doesn't always listen to Spirit because the ego busies his mind with distractions. But son, the spiritual realm is not separate from the physical realm. What is physical is but a concentration of what is spiritual; a spirit-concentrate. Man's life is a physical experience of the self-same spiritual, son."

Seeker: "Father, if the intellect and memory are part and parcel of man's psyche, what is the issue?"

Abbot: "No issue, son. Only the ego."

Seeker: "What of the ego?"

Abbot: "The ego does not spring forth from the wholesomeness of the spirit of mind. It is the issue because it projects itself onto the whole and makes a travesty of man, of his love and his nature."

Seeker: "Are we not what we know and can remember? Is our memory not who we are?"

Abbot: "Who you are? Yes, that's your ego, but not what you are, son."

Seeker: "Please explain father."

Abbot: "The ego is malleable. Who you are is changeable. But what you are is wholesome, unchanging, undying, and eternal. The sweet innocence and joy of childhood is archetypal of 'what' you are and this is before 'who' you become, the ego, which is given to you by your society and culture. Draw yourself inward, son, and cast your mind back and forth to see for yourself what I am trying to illustrate. Do you see how your very name, a sound people make to call your attention gradually becomes verbose with many attributes and attachments over the years?"

Seeker: "Yes I do, father."

Abbot: "Do you see how it acquires these attributes? From your family and cultural traditions, your academic information and qualifications to your titles and achievements?"

Seeker: "Yes I do, father."

Abbot: "Do you see how a simple and beautiful childhood becomes weighty over time with the objects of attachments?"

Seeker: "Yes I do, father."

Abbot: "Do you see how a spacious and free mind fills up with the data of your acculturation, your academic knowledge, your histories, your wishes, hopes, beliefs, and all the other ornaments of the ego?"

Seeker: "Yes I do, father."

Abbot: "Do you see how in the prime years of man, his achievements and possessions become the cornerstones of his identity and source of pleasure and pride?"

Seeker: "Yes I do, father."

Abbot: "Do you see how he is heralded by his society for his achievements and possessions and how he is envied by his fellow men?"

Seeker: "Yes I do, father."

Abbot: "Do you see how man's covetousness develops and is fanned by his society and envy of others?"

Seeker: "Yes I do, father."

Abbot: "Do you see how he strives and competes with his fellow men to gather those achievements and possessions to decorate his ego personality?"

Seeker: "Yes I do, father."

Abbot: "Do you see how men relate with one another through their egos and from their egoistic minds?"

Seeker: "Yes I do, father."

Abbot: "Do you see how feisty the ego is and how man has no leisure to seek self-knowledge?"

Seeker: "Yes I do, father."

Abbot: "Do you see his source of pleasure and pride, and for which reason, he proclaims it and by extension his culture over others and humanity?"

Seeker: "Yes I do, father."

Abbot: "Do you see how intertwined man's factors of division are and why man eats man?"

Seeker: "Yes I do, father."

Abbot: "Do you see why the ego's death ought to be celebrated?"

Seeker: "Alas, I do, father."

Abbot: "Ah, the beauty of seeing yourself by yourself for yourself. Again son, do you see how in the sunset years of man, his intellect loses its feistiness and his memory atrophies?"

Seeker: "Yes I do, father."

Abbot: "Do you see how a once pleasurable and prideful ego decays from the brain and the child is born again in old age?"

Seeker: "Yes I do, father."

Abbot: "Do you see how malleable and fleeting memory is?"

Seeker: "Yes I do, father."

Abbot: "Do you see how short-lived the ego is? Do you see that it is the ego that has a personality that is divided from other personalities, a family that is divided from other families, a nationalism that is divided from other nationalisms, an ideology that is divided from other ideologies, a belief which is divided from other beliefs, etc.?"

Seeker: "Indeed, father. Does the ego survive death? Will man carry his earthly identity and mental accumulation into the afterlife?"

Abbot: "No, son. The signs for this are clear to see in a man's old age and if one were to live long enough, he'd see for himself. Man's memories are stored in the cells of his brain and surely, the cells are subject to decay and death. What survives his death are the immutable and eternal energies of his soul. Ah, the joy of eternity my son."

Seeker: "I am mystified by this, father. You mean the name, the family, the achievements and titles, the experiences, the beliefs, and the rest, all end in the death of the body?"

Abbot: "Absolutely, son. Don't be mystified by small matters. Be mystified by what lies yonder. Only souls go through the holy gate of death; man's memories remain behind together with the rest of his mortal remains."

Seeker: "Surely, father, our pious deeds must be in the records of Heaven, for what will inform and guarantee our admission there?"

Abbot: "What are some of those deeds you call pious and the doing of which should earn you admission into Heaven? And remember, there's only one deed, son, it is love. Also remember, your pilgrimages and rituals, your sectarian beliefs and dogmas are the impious fetters of your divisive cultures. There can be only one God and one Heaven and Heaven has no ink for small affairs."

Seeker: "What about man's love? What about his compassion and kindness towards others? What about the charity and the alms we give to the needy? What about the good we do for society which does not come from the ego but from man's honest and genuine efforts?"

Abbot: "You have just enumerated some of the characteristics of man's true nature, son. Do you covet a reward for being true to your nature? Should the Sun ask for a reward for shining its life-giving light on Earth? Should the Oceans ask for a reward for rising and falling as rain? Should the bees ask for a reward for pollinating your plants? Should the Earth ask for a reward for carrying the lot of you on her back for all these years? Should the other planets ask for a reward for keeping Earth in balance? Why does man covet a reward in the name of Heaven?

If you must seek Heaven, see to it that you remain true to your nature and wholesome in your deeds; for what lies yonder remains to be seen by each soul. Ah, the pains of foolish covetousness my son."

Seeker: "At least father, man will be remembered after he has died. Posterity shall honor him; his children and descendants will shower his tomb with flowers and prayers. He will long be credited for his achievement and contribution to society; his works shall be praised and displayed in our halls of fame. A man may die but his legacy will live on. Is this not worth his sweat?"

Abbot: "What is worthwhile does not require his sweat; only his love. What is worthwhile enriches his life and that of those around him, while he still breathes. What is worthwhile does not require public approval or recognition. What is worthwhile are living and effervescent flowers; for dead flowers and stale words mean nothing to the dead nor Heaven. Look through your history books and halls of fame to note all those who are honored and ask yourself how they benefit from your remembrances and praises.

What causes man to be so jittery about the afterlife that he tears down the world, to live on after, either through Heaven or legacy? How can something you don't know frighten you so terribly? If man were wiser than he pretends to be, his legacy would be to give all his love and leave a more loving world. Properties and accolades are subject to the heavy winds of time my son, remember. Ah, the weight of the ego my son."

Seeker: "I am shaken up by your words father. But still, Heaven and Hell are motivational drivers in the lives and actions of billions of people, can you please elucidate on this?"

Abbot: "Heaven and Hell are to children what pleasure and pain are to adults. The wonderment of this is why adults want to be children, my son. Why do they still need to be encouraged to be on good behavior and be rewarded with Heaven or be punished in Hell for bad behavior? Why do adults prefer the comforts of bedtime stories and treats than to take their own lives into their own hands? Why do adults abandon their inner sanctuary and ask stupid questions and why are they so eager to be answered, to be deceived? And again son, why does man wear his illusions so fondly and proudly?"

Seeker: "Is it because man believes his illusions to be the truth, and does not wish to be told otherwise, and to be proven wrong?"

Abbot: "Indeed, son, it is as you say. And, because man prefers the amusement park of ignorance and fears the responsibility of his free will. Ah, the illusion of believing and the deception of man."

Seeker: "Indeed, father. So, there is no Heaven and Hell?"

Abbot: "Not in the sense of your sectarian dogmatic claims, son."

Seeker: "So the good will not reap Heaven nor the bad burn in Hell?"

Abbot: "Again son, what happens in the afterlife remains to be seen by each soul. Any speculations and dogmatic claims can be safely dispensed with."

Seeker: "So what should be the motivation for being good?"

Abbot: "You cannot have a motive for being good my son. It is what you are. Remember, the Sun does not ask for motivation, neither do the little busy bees."

Seeker: "So a person can choose to be bad and wicked unto his fellow men since what happens after his death is his own business?"

Abbot: "They might burn alone."

Seeker: "But you said there's no Hell."

Abbot: "Yes, but it remains to be seen by each soul. Also, if they are bad and wicked unto their fellow men, they are equally bad and wicked unto themselves. And the evil they do to the world; they do to themselves for posterity shall inherit its damages. And who is posterity if not the self-same mankind? Harken to my words oh son."

Seeker: "What about judgment in the afterlife?"

Abbot: "That too remains to be seen in the afterlife by each soul."

Seeker: "Father, I am flabbergasted because this is completely diagonal to what man is told by the religious currents on Earth. Ancient scriptures have told of God-men, figures purported to be incarnations of God in human form, who had come to Earth with knowledge and admonitions about Heaven and Hell, and how souls are judged and segregated into them based on their faiths and deeds on Earth. Tell me, father, were they wrong? Is there such a thing as God-man? Does the one God take human form to guide His children?"

Abbot: "Son, what happens in the afterlife remains to be seen by each soul and cannot be told by another, no matter who they were. The one God and indeed the Great Circle took human form, and ever since Adam, the Earth has been trodden by innumerable billions of His forms. You are all guides unto one another with your love, and where a brother falls and lags, lift him with your love; be your brother's keeper for you are all Adam. But son, I suppose your question is still regarding mediumship. That is, man on Earth and God in Heaven and the relationship between them, is that not so?"

Seeker: "Yes father."

Abbot: "I understand, son, the mist and dust of this illusion are thick and require some more effort. Remember son, the separation of God and man, and the objectification of God in the heavens is what gives persistence to the grand deception. Remember also, that what makes man human is not without him but within him. If you must know, son, then know this, man is unto the Divine; eyes and ears; hands and legs; minds and hearts. Harken to my words oh son."

Seeker: "Father, you mean God sees and hears through man?"

Abbot: "Yes, and through innumerable eyes and ears. What the Divine can see through the eyes of falcons, it cannot see through the eyes of man. What the Divine can hear through the ears of bats, it cannot hear through the ears of sheep. Where the Divine can walk with the legs of millipedes, it cannot go there with the legs of elephants. Where the Divine can fly to with the wings of cicadas, it cannot get there with the wings of doves. It is so. All are in service of the Great Circle my son."

Seeker: "Is man the same as God?"

Abbot: "Son, the word God in your imperfect earthly language is loose and used in varied contexts. Man does not yet have a word to describe the Great Circle in fullness. The Great Circle underlies everything including man; in their infinity, in their unity, in their humanity, in their love, and their oneness and wholeness. Son, do not pay heed to any sectarian claims that reduce God into human skins; that appropriates God for their cultural supremacy over others; that divide man against man; that enforce hierarchies amongst men, for you are all gods, divine and complete, to the last and least of you."

Seeker: "And who sits on the Heavenly throne and is bowed to by servant angels and principalities?"

Abbot: "The Great Circle has no inclinations to trivialities and vanities. These are bedtime stories for children, invented by crafty minds."

Seeker: "Father, you mean our sacred scriptures are inventions? Why are they said to be sacred then?"

Abbot: "They are proclaimed so by their inventors; but does it make them so? What is sacred is permanent, unchanging, and undying. Ten thousand scriptures have come and gone but what is sacred still reigns in the heart of man. Many epochs before yours had not yet learned to write; are the writers of your scriptures so arrogant as to bastardize their existence and divinity? Son ground yourself in the timeless and endless gaping void of silence and let external sources of knowledge become obsolete."

Seeker: "Father, can you please dissect the grand deception? It seems to me a lot depends on it and therefore, having a good grasp of it would be helpful to my quest for wisdom."

Abbot: "Son, the grand deception is a leviathan of mammoth influence in the lives of people, which lurks in the background and weaves itself into everything. You are right, to understand it is to gain clarity and ignite the torch to self-understanding. The leviathan has survived for millennia because it is fed and nourished by men who suckle milk from its innumerable breasts and are in turn nourished by it. Those men have come to depend on the leviathan for their pomp and pride and the leviathan has come to depend on them for its subsistence. They need each other to survive; without the leviathan, its children would die and without its children, the leviathan would die.

Son, the leviathan has many tentacles. The first tentacle is 'God the Human Being' or what is popularly called theology. This is man's daring attempt to define and describe the Divine based on a personhood and following from that erroneous premise, he assigns characteristics to it. But what man assigns to the Divine as a matter of fact must emanate from his thinking and therefore, not perfect, and not true. He does this using positive statements such as the Divine has a personality, the Divine has a name, the Divine has a Gender, etc. but anything that is produced from man's thinking reflects himself. Therefore, since man loves vanity, the supposed personality of the Divine, God, must also love vanity and so, he sets up an altar to prostrate to Him while forgetting that what he worships is his own projection. Son, if man wishes to think of the Divine in human terms as a person, for his convenience and ease of cognition, then may we entreat him to speak of God and indeed, the Divine in apophasis and not in the trouble-laden and deceptive positive assertions that he heaves on the Divine innocence.

The second tentacle of the leviathan is the invention of 'The Devil as the enemy of God and man'. The third tentacle of the leviathan is the supposed mediumship between man and his maker; for which reason whisperers and institutions exist to be the link, and to claim to guide man to the Divine. But son, a man needs nothing outside his circle as I have already told you.

The fourth tentacle of the leviathan is 'God's chosen people' or racism as sanctioned by God's favoritism. Son, Intelligence is absolute as I have already told you and what even God does must conform to its dictates as it is indispensable and integral to Oneness. Where intelligence and love are present, can there be division, favoritism, and enmity?

The second, third, and fourth tentacles of the leviathan of the grand deception are not very strong and depend on the truthfulness or falsity of the first tentacle. Son, your quest for wisdom must be fulfilled by yourself and it is only then that your wisdom would be pristine and impeccable. Reside in silence and let holy understanding come to you and feed you with its nuggets of wisdom.

Another strong tentacle of the leviathan, the fifth, is 'man the sinful infant'. This assumption has contributed enormously to the subsistence of the grand deception. It is the belief that man's soul is defective, sinful, and incomplete which is brought to Earth to correct its defect and incompleteness. Some go as far as to claim that man could become God through multiple lifetimes of continuous perfection. But son, as I have already told you, man's soul is perfect, complete, and eternal, just like the Divine itself. The process of becoming implies that you're adding to that which is becoming or rearing the soul of man through time and knowledge. Man likes to refer to the example of a child who knows nothing at first but then grows up to be matured and wise in later years as evidence that in multiple lifetimes, the soul could expand and become grandiose with some kind of powers. But son, it is grandly erroneous to suppose that the soul of the child is lesser than the soul of the man. What the man becomes in later years is a mere accumulation or gathering of information from the outside.

The child may not fear fire today but tomorrow he will learn that fire burns, it doesn't mean the soul has become wiser for the child has merely acquired information. The child may be innocent today and when a man, becomes corrupted by his culture, it doesn't mean the soul has become corrupted for the man has merely acquired an ego. The soul is always pristine, complete, and eternal; it doesn't become anything either in a single lifetime or multiple lifetimes. Son, understanding this tentacle of the Leviathan would aid you a lot in your quest for wisdom. Reside in silence.

The sixth tentacle of the leviathan is belief. It could be belief in atheism, theism, pantheism, materialism, immaterialism, mythology, and other similar grand claims; belief takes away man's attention and intelligence and denies him of perception. It blinds him to the simple shelter of truth that is before his very eyes and he holds on to castles in the air.

The seventh tentacle of the leviathan is culture, which buttresses and promotes the other tentacles. The eighth tentacle is the search for or belief in external spiritual powers or blessings through either religious practices or sorcery. Son, all spiritual powers, and blessings emanate from within man himself; for no other person nor entity can confer anything on the soul of man. But the ego cowers in fear and seeks external validation of its so-called security. The ninth tentacle is the concept of Heaven and Hell. Son, I will tell you more about these tentacles later but as I have already told you, wisdom comes from within you. Reside in silence."

Seeker: "Indeed, father. Could you please explain what speaking of God in apophasis means?"

Abbot: "Son, how big and powerful is the one God or the Divine if you like?"

Seeker: "I do not know, father."

Abbot: "Correct, son. So, you can only describe it in apophasis and say He is all-big, all-powerful, or omnipotent, and all-pervading. Again, where is the one God located in place and time?"

Seeker: "I do not know, father."

Abbot: "Correct, son, you cannot also know. He is omnipresent and all-pervading. Again, who are the chosen people of God?"

Seeker: "I do not know, father."

Abbot: "Correct, son. All men are children of God and chosen by God. Again, son, what is God's religion and scripture?"

Seeker: "I do not know, father."

Abbot: "Correct, son. He has none and all religions and scriptures kowtow to the truth. Son, apophasis is to negate and deny falsities in perceiving what is true and is inspired by the love of truth or holy doubt. When man men speak in positive assertions about what is unknown and cannot be known through his finite perception, they engage in fantasy."

Seeker: "Father your words are laden with substance and beckons more questions. Please tell me more about the nature of the afterlife?"

Abbot: "Son, a whale could swim across the oceans and tell you everything about the deepest sea but cannot know a thing about what happens on land. A lion could brave the jungles and tell you everything about the wilderness but cannot know a thing about the sky. An eagle could fly and perch on clouds and sing about the glorious skies but cannot know what happens in a honeycomb. Bees could navigate the catacombs of a honeycomb but cannot know what happens in an anthill. It is so. Man could wish to know everything about the world but cannot know what happens beyond the holy gate of death.

Only fish can tell you about the oceans; only beasts can tell you about the wilderness; only birds can tell you about the skies; only bees can tell you about the intricacies of a honeycomb and only ants can drag through the tiny aisles of an anthill and bring you, the royal commands of their queen. It is so. Only souls can tell you about the afterlife and if man wishes to know; only the holy gate of death can reveal what happens in the afterlife. Only the dead can know what happens to the dead. The living may make assumptions, and comfort themselves with a myriad of imaginations and fantasies but only the dead know death, my son. Burn those books that claim to know what happens in the afterlife and shut those mouths that claim to speak of it. Castigate and shun the company of those who give you promises for the afterlife, for even they, are yet to see it."

Seeker: "Is the afterlife akin to Morpheus? For you said only souls arrive here."

Abbot: "Morpheus is part of life and a soul in life is laden with the limitations of the flesh. Death is the ultimate end of life and it frees the soul of weight to pass through its holy gate. Man cannot know unless he makes the journey but he wishes to know otherwise and so theories spring up like serpents; hissing melodious songs."

Seeker: "Father, does man pass to oblivion when he dies?"

Abbot: "Does man suppose he comes from oblivion when he is born? Why does he not ask about where he comes from with the same zeal and ardor as he does about where he goes after death? Remember son, man is like a circle; complete and eternal. And when he asks about the afterlife, who asks? Is it the ego or the soul?"

Seeker: "Tell me, father."

Abbot: "The soul has no cause to ask about death; for it knows only existence. That which asks is that which is afraid to die, to end. Ah, the fears of the ego my son."

Seeker: "The ego again?"

Abbot: "Yes, son. The ego accumulates and hoards its achievements and possessions. The ego develops attachments to its things, people, and places. The ego pleasures and prides itself and says to others that it loves itself. The ego doesn't want to lose its possessions. The ego fears to come to an end. The ego covets continuity; either heaven or legacy. Beware of the ego and its wishes my son."

Seeker: "Father, is man composed of two separate persons? You speak of the ego as though it were a separate entity."

Abbot: "No, son. Man is unitary and wholesome in his originality. The ego is not a separate entity but develops and comes into operation as a child of memory and uses the intellect to function. The ego exists completely in time and death is the end of a person's time in a single lifetime. But the essence of man, the soul, lives in existence, in timelessness. The ego always changes with time, my son.

You can draw inwardly and cast your mind back and forth to see for yourself how the ego evolves with time. Do you see how a person could be one personality in their early adulthood and a decade later become a completely different personality with children, more friends, more wealth, more titles, more respect, etc.?"

Seeker: "Yes, father I see."

Abbot: "And do you see how another decade that passes could thrust this same person into a different personality of misery, poverty, and shame?"

Seeker: "Yes, father I see."

Abbot: "And do you see how another decade that passes could uplift this same person from misery to happiness and pleasures?"

Seeker: "Yes, father I see."

Abbot: "Such is the nature of the ego my son. It changes with time and must end when the time of that person's lifetime is over. But that's not really what they were all along, for time and seasons change but the soul remains rooted in a timeless and a measureless dimension."

Seeker: "Where is this dimension? Is it in the heavens?"

Abbot: "It is everywhere, son. Man calls it Existence."

Seeker: "Is it in the physical universe?"

Abbot: "The physical universe is the tip of the iceberg of Existence. It is what man can see my son. Morpheus is part of life but do you see Morpheus when awake? It is only when you retire from your physicality that Morpheus becomes alive, is that not so?"

Seeker: "Yes, father it is."

Abbot: "Your waking life cannot deny the existence of Morpheus and Morpheus cannot deny the existence of your waking life. It is so. They both exist in life. Also, birth cannot deny death and death cannot deny birth. It is so. Both birth and death occur in Existence; a timeless and measureless Oneness."

Seeker: "Father, please tell me more about birth and death?"

Abbot: "Son, to understand birth and death, you must first understand Existence, in which they occur. And yet, your finite mind can't grasp what it is because your senses are sorely open to only a minuscule of Existence. You cannot measure Existence, nor can you conceptualize it. You cannot describe Existence, neither can you imagine it. You can only be in it and feel it for yourself when you enter the silence of being."

Seeker: "Father, kindly indulge me, in simple terms."

Abbot: "Existence is the Totality of totalities. Existence is the Being of beings. Existence is everything; there's nothing outside its circumference for there's no circumference. Existence is timeless; there's nothing before it and nothing after it for time itself occurs within it."

Seeker: "Father, I am following you so far, kindly go on."

Abbot: "Matter and therefore materiality is a potentiality within Existence. Materiality as a potentiality in Existence could emerge or materialize as stars and their solar systems, galaxies, and indeed as universes. Materiality as a potentiality in Existence could emerge or materialize as planets and their attributes. Materiality as a potentiality in Existence could emerge or materialize as living things. And yet materialization is not an isolated process, for it combines with innumerable potentialities and qualities to become existent. Do you follow, son?"

Seeker: "Absolutely, father. What are some of the other potentialities and qualities of Existence?"

Abbot: "Beingness is its primary quality. Thingness is its primary potentiality. Consciousness and Love are also her qualities. Life and elementals are also her potentialities."

Seeker: "What is man, per these qualities and potentialities?"

Abbot: "He is a living thing because his body is composed of matter and Life. And a being because his soul is composed of self-awareness, consciousness, and love."

Seeker: "What about animals and plants, father?"

Abbot: "Animals comprising all faunas are indeed living things as they have matter and life. It is the same for plants comprising all floras. They also have lower expressions of consciousness and love. Only man has self-awareness because he and his maker are one."

Seeker: "Father, do animals have self-awareness at all?"

Abbot: "Lower expressions, my son. Only man was uplifted from the animal kingdom and set on the pedestal of the Divine. Only Adam was chosen. Only Adam knows 'I' and can say 'I am'. Only Adam was brought out of a horrible pit and the miry clay of the Earth and his feet were set on a rock. Only Adam's hands work the dictates of his maker and his heart. And you are all Adam, my son."

Seeker: "Was Adam molded from clay and breathed into?"

Abbot: "Adam is not his body, but his soul. Matter is a potentiality within Existence; a tedious and meticulous process, and when his material potential was achieved, he was lifted and became Adam. So that through him Existence may shepherd its creations for the glory of all."

Seeker: "Is the tedious and meticulous process the same as our concept of evolution?"

Abbot: "How else can a potential be achieved?"

Seeker: "Indeed, father. So, creation was not done in six days?"

Abbot: "Whether six days, six years, or six million years; time and matter are relative in Existence. Only Beingness is absolute, now, and always."

Seeker: "You mean Existence?"

Abbot: "Yes, son. Touche!"

Seeker: "Please father can you give me a simile for Existence and Life?"

Abbot: "Imagine a lone universe, with a lone galaxy, with a lone star, with a lone planet, and on the planet also, imagine a lone giant tree, with a size-less width, and a sky-less height, with infinite branches and leaves, and covered atop the leaves that surround the globular tree are so many beautiful flowers with vibrance, fragrance, and nectar. Can you see this in your mind's eye, son?"

Seeker: "Indeed, as clearly as you describe it, father."

Abbot: "Great, son. The lone mighty globular tree represents the physical world sprouting out of the dark nothingness and somethingness of Existence which is the lone planet and its galactic system. At the very top of the tree are the beautiful flowers which represent Life. Indeed, Life is a great potentiality of Existence, therefore making Earth a unique experience by Spirit through Its Creation.

Son, is the total essence of the Earth not in the root of the mighty tree that precipitated from it? Is the total essence of the root not in the trunk that precipitated from it? Is the total essence of the trunk not in the branch that precipitated from it? Is the total essence of the branch not in the leaf that precipitated from it? Is the total essence of the leaf not in the flower that precipitated from it? Is the total essence of the flower not in the seed that precipitated from it? Is the total essence of the Universe, the Galaxy, the Star, the Earth, the tree, its leaves, and flowers not contained in the teeny-weeny seed of Life? And son, if you could see all this in your mind's eye as truthfully as daylight, have you not arrived at something incalculably great? Harken to my words oh son."

Seeker: "What about in-animate or nonliving-things?"

Abbot: "In-animate things are also matter. Everything is a living thing; with varying degrees of beingness and thingness. Beingness is the primary quality of a thing that exists and thingness is the objective quality about a thing that exists."

Seeker: "Father, can you give me some examples to help unfreeze my mind?"

Abbot: "A piece of stone has a high degree of thingness but has a low degree of beingness. Its thingness can be objectively perceived from the perspective of man. Its beingness cannot be objectively perceived from the perspective of man because he looks with his naked eyes. Its beingness could be easily perceived if the gross matter that weighs it down were stripped off, my son. Microbes, having no gross matter discernible by human eyes, have a low degree of thingness but have beingness and therefore exist. It is so."

Seeker: "Father, you said thingness is the objective quality about a thing that exists?"

Abbot: "Yes, son."

Seeker: "Is it from the objective perspective of man?"

Abbot: "A thing exists whether or not a man can objectively discern it."

Seeker: "Like microbes and elementals?"

Abbot: "Yes and other innumerable things that are not yet discernible by the limited senses of man."

Seeker: "Father, you said a man and his maker are one, could you please explain this?"

Abbot: "Man's primary quality is beingness even before he materializes his thingness in the form of the human body; for in the beginning was the son and the son became flesh and he was called Adam. The primary essences of beingness are consciousness and love. Out of the effulgence of his consciousness, beams his love, his humanity. Out of the plenitude of his love, the world revolves around him and bends to his will. The animals flock after him and the clouds tail his crop fields; the planets carry him across the cosmos, the stars brighten his daytime and the moons are lanterns for his nighttime; he is nourished by the plants and rivers; and the birds sing to wake him up each morning. Ah, what a wonderful thing he is."

Seeker: "Indeed, father. Tell me more."

Abbot: "He has self-awareness and can say 'I am', and because he is, and is self-aware, he creates and because he creates, his potentialities are innumerable just like Existence itself, out of which he materialized. Have you not heard them say a man is a microcosm of the macrocosm?"

Seeker: "Indeed, father. But can man's artificial creations be likened to the creations of the Divine, I mean Existence?"

Abbot: "Not nearly, son. However, it is not the products of creation that matter but rather the art and act of creation; which is in man also. Has man not left the squalor and chills of the caves to the greenery and flowery of the gardens and orchards to dominate land? Has man's handiwork not conquered the depths of the Oceans? Has man not burst out of the shield of his environment and ventured into Space? Has man not split the atom? Ah, the wonders of limitless potentialities my son."

Seeker: "How does man's creations compare to those of Existence?"

Abbot: "Is man not an extension of Existence?"

Seeker: "He is, father."

Abbot: "Surely then, son, his creations are also in service of the trajectory and potentialities of Existence itself. Man may go wrong but Existence course-corrects his path and his world, and ultimately, man serves the cause of his maker. Can man have any wishes or desires and can he do anything outside the confines of Existence?"

Seeker: "Father, you said Existence has no confines."

Abbot: "Correct, son."

Seeker: "Father, is the beingness of man the same as the Beingness of Existence?"

Abbot: "Son, the Beingness of Existence descends into its creation and takes numerous forms including the beingness of man. But the total Beingness of Existence is uncreated and beyond the realm of man's consciousness and understanding. When created in man, it becomes sense-enabled and because it senses, it is conscious and self-aware; for that which cannot sense cannot be conscious nor self-aware. The act of sensing is a phenomenon that occurs in the world of creation; which is below the Beingness of Existence."

Seeker: "But animals also have senses, father."

Abbot: "Animals have up to five senses, the physical senses but man has in addition to the physical senses, a sixth and a seventh. The holy spirit of the mind of man and the love of the heart of man. Together, these two higher senses of man give him a rich inner experience. The mind tunes into the higher frequencies of the Divine and his love reflects and beams his divinity."

Seeker: "But animals also have brains and hearts."

Abbot: "Son, I am not referring to the physiological uses of a brain and a heart but rather, their metaphysical qualities."

Seeker: "Indeed, father. What about men who distrust the truth of the metaphysical or spiritual realm and insist the world is purely material? What about the so-called atheists who demand evidence of the existence or veracity of the Divine before they can accept it? How does the mind of such people work, father?"

Abbot: "Son, indeed, many men have tended to distrust in the veracity of the Divine due to their approach of perception. It is like a sugar asking a sugarcane plant to prove that it produces sugar; while forgetting that it is the evidence it seeks. It is like the mustard seed asking the mustard plant to prove that it is a mustard; while forgetting that it is the evidence it seeks. It is like salt demanding of the Ocean to prove that it produces salt; while forgetting that it is the evidence it seeks.

It is like water saying to itself that it is thirsty; without knowing that it is the quencher it seeks. It is like fire saying to itself that it is hot; without knowing that it is in its nature to be hot. It is like the clouds weeping for turning into rain; without knowing that it is only taking a trip and will be back home soon enough. It is like the eyes saying they cannot see themselves; while forgetting to look inwardly. Indeed, son, it is like ignorance saying to itself that truth is a lie. It is self-deception. It is so. Ah, belief, you are the comforter of the ignorant, flee and let men be free.

Son, man's cultures with all their words, dogmas, mythologies, cosmologies, theories, theologies and what have you, present a narrative and depiction of the Divine that cause doubt in the minds of people, and only demand blind faith but man is a rational being, made so by his maker to guide his free will, and therefore must question. But logic, like belief, cannot apply to the domain of the Divine because the Divine is beyond measurement. The man of logic is stingy with his intelligence because he hangs on just one aspect of its domains, logic. Were he to rise above the rung of logic and ascend its limitations, he would know better and not drag the Divine into the arena of thought and its feistiness."

Seeker: "Indeed, father. Can we now talk about birth and death?"

Abbot: "Yes, son, and, life and afterlife. There are four supremacies of Existence, they are; birth, life, death, and afterlife. Everything that has beingness must phase through these supremacies as a matter of course, my son."

Seeker: "Father, I am eager for your words. Do you mean phase through them in the fashion of a continuum?"

Abbot: "Yes, son but not chronologically. For what begins doesn't end and what ends only begins. They are phases and yet intertwined; they are perceivably separate and yet whole. They are the Supreme Lords and all must bow to them; they are the four legs of the seat of Existence. Harken to my words oh son."

Seeker: "Indeed father, I am. Please go on."

Abbot: "What lives that was not born? What dies that did not live? What is born that was not dead?"

Seeker: "I humbly defer to your wisdom, father."

Abbot: "Universes are born and live and die. Galaxies are born and live and die. Stars are born and live and die. Planets are born and live and die. Living things are born and live and die. It is so. Man too, is born and lives and dies. But son, though living things die from physical existence; what causes the birth of living things exists always, beyond the physical world of mortals and may precipitate in and out of life. Everything dies but nothing dies, harken to my words oh son."

Seeker: "Father, what about the elements?"

Abbot: "Son, chemical elements do not have reality in themselves; only potentiality. They are always in a state of potentiality until joined with others to create living things. They may combine themselves to become water, air, fire, or earth and these in turn populate the physical universe. So, in living things, they are born and live and die. Everything dies but nothing dies."

Seeker: "What makes stars and galaxies living things?"

Abbot: "Life is what occurs between birth and death; and needn't necessarily be biological. Stars are born and die; galaxies are equally born and die. What happens between the holy gates of birth and death is a living process and has a purpose. For the thingness of Existence is driven by purposefulness and everything that exists in life longs after its purpose. A galaxy longs to be home to stars and planets; a star longs to produce its radiation; a rock longs to build; water longs to produce life; mockingbirds long to sing; lovers long to love. It is so."

Seeker: "What about a thing that exists in the afterlife, what does it long after?"

Abbot: "Man cannot know all its longings but one thing is certain, it yearns for life, my son. Life is a potentiality of the afterlife and purposefulness is the object of Life. It is so."

Seeker: "But why die only to long after life again?"

Abbot: "Life has innumerable variety of expressions my son. Amoeba has life and purpose. Man has life and purpose. Are the lives of man and amoeba the same and can they have the same purposes? Again son, even amongst men; a male's purpose is not the same as that of a female and a farmer's purpose is not the same as a cobbler's. It is so."

Seeker: "Indeed, it is, father. Please tell me more about Man's purpose."

Abbot: "Man has the unique ability and divine capacity to define his purpose, my son. Stars and planets have fixed purposes. Also, faunas and floras have fixed purposes but a man may yet choose his own. Man's purpose is limitless because his creativity has limitless potentialities. Harken to my words oh son."

Seeker: "Father, can we talk about birth and death as they relate to man?"

Abbot: "Yes, but before that let's look at life and the afterlife from the perspective of man. Life is known to man but the afterlife is shut to him. He is of relatively a small stature and yet he lives in a mammoth world in an ever-expanding universe. He has limitless creativity and potential and yet he lives in a society that imposes on his limitlessness. He longs for community and relationships, and yet he suffers them. He yearns for freedom and yet he is caged in a culture that clips his wings and fetters him to traditions and customs."

Seeker: "Father, but life is not all miserable as you have just painted it to be."

Abbot: "Yes, son, it is not. Man's life is certainly not without its treats and perks; like caged birds enjoying a meal of grains tossed at them. It is also true that not all birds have lost the use of their wings and not all men have lost the use of their minds. Whereas most birds live their lives in the sweet wild of nature; most men are caged. Whereas you need a meshed cage for birds; you only need to cage man's mind, a far easier feat than trapping birds into a cage. Being caged and having lost his freedom; suffering his sorrows and contending with the travails of life; feeling despair and hopelessness; he looks up to the heavens with teary eyes and begs to know the unknowable, the afterlife. Ah, what agony man has made of his life my son."

Seeker: "Father, will his desperation and quest to know what pertains in the afterlife ever be achieved?"

Abbot: "Yes, but not while he lives. Remember son, only the holy gate of death shall reveal to man the Great Unknown in the afterlife."

Seeker: "So death is a journey into the unknown?"

Abbot: "Yes. All that lives must live to maturity and fecundity of its purpose and must succumb to the supremacy of death. Old cornstalks must be harvested and cut down to give way for new seeds to grow; death is the sublimation of the old so that the new may live. It is so. And what lives that was not dead?"

Seeker: "Indeed, father. What about birth?"

Abbot: "That which lives must be regenerated after the fashion and manner of its kind. Like begets like; man begets man; corn begets corn; and so forth, my son. For living things do not magically precipitate; they are meticulously regenerated into physical existence through the holy gate of birth."

Seeker: "Father, why do you refer to birth and death as holy?"

Abbot: "Yes, they are, and, life and afterlife. They are the four holy supremacies of Existence. From birth through life to death and the afterlife and all over again in a cyclical loop; the Great Circle binds them together in Existence. Like the Sunrise of morning for Birth, like the vicissitudes of day-time for Life, like the Sunset of evening for Death, and like the quietude and rest of night-time for Afterlife, and all over again the next day and for infinity, man rides on in majesty in the palm of God the Birther, God the Sustainer, God the Deather and God the Restorer. Harken to my words oh son."

Seeker: "Father, what is the meaning of life?"

Abbot: "Son, everything that exists is fashioned for a purpose. Meaning is derived from the fulfillment of a thing's purpose. Man, too must choose his purpose based on the necessities of his environment and the wisdom of his mind and heart. In pursuance of a peaceful and purposeful life, he finds meaning. In being true to his nature, he loves and in loving, he finds meaning with his intelligence and his compassion. In following the dictates of a weightless heart and an egoless mind, he finds meaning. And with integrity in his heart, his ambition is truer to the collective good and unity of the world. And indeed son, in achieving the collective destiny of man through cooperation and unity, he fulfills his purpose and finds peace and joy; the meaning of his life."

Seeker: "Father, what is the difference between purpose and meaning of life?"

Abbot: "Son, the purpose of a spoon is to fetch morsels of food into the mouth but the meaning of using a spoon is to feel civilized. The purpose of a vehicle is to carry and transport people but the meaning of using a vehicle is convenience and expediency. The purpose of a thing is driven by its utility and the meaning of the utility of a thing can only be derived by an intelligent actor. Son, whereas the purpose of a thing is more direct and more conspicuous, the meaning is more abstract and seeks virtue; requiring the holy spirit of the mind and love to lead man to it.

Son, I already told you that man's purpose is limitless and within the leeway of his free will. A man could purpose his gifts to grow crops and livestock for the needs of his small village and derive contentment and fulfillment and therefore meaning from living a life's purpose that nourishes life and people. Man could also become a cosmonaut traversing unknown distances and places to help mankind understand their physical world better and may equally feel great about the meaning of his life. It is not about which is greater or lesser my son, it is about being centered in self-knowledge to know what to do by yourself.

But son, man wants to be told what his purpose is and what meaning to look for in life by his numerous authorities and he gladly follows."

Seeker: "Am I to take from the foregoing that man is not born with a destiny cast in stone? Is a man not fated for a cause or purpose beyond his wishes or control?"

Abbot: "Son, man is fated for a purpose which he must choose through his own divine-given volition. The Great Circle does not limit limitlessness; it does not give with the right hand and take back with the left hand. Man must choose and it is in the choosing that he may find meaning. For that which cannot choose cannot find meaning; goats and sheep cannot find meaning. And if man chooses evil then agony and putrefaction shall be his portion, and if he chooses good, then he shall find peace and joy, the meaning of his life. Ah, the dilemma of freewill my son."

Seeker: "Father, does a man have free will?"

Abbot: "Free will is the basis of his creativity and limitlessness. Free will is the basis of his completeness and his wholesomeness. Free will is the bedrock of a man's individuality. It is the instrument that underpins his originality of thought and point of view of the world. It is the bond between the lover and the beloved. Son, a thing cannot be in a state of completeness and wholesomeness if it cannot act on its own accord and therefore, free will, my son."

Seeker: "Tell me more, father."

Abbot: "Can man express his love without freewill? If man was forced by nature to love, would that still qualify to be called love?"

Seeker: "Indeed not, father."

Abbot: "Correct, son. When there's love there must also be freedom; for the Divine so loves the world that He gave His begotten sons free will as a token of His love for them. It is this same freedom man gives to his beloved when he does not seek to possess her and does not also seek to bend her to his will, and that is called true love. And isn't the beloved's reciprocal love inflamed by that sense of freedom, of not being possessed and yet bursting with the yearning for Oneness with the lover?"

Seeker: "Indeed, father, it does inflame love towards Oneness."

Abbot: "Again, son, can man find meaning in life without free will? If man was conscripted to act for the collective good, could he find fulfillment, peace, and joy?"

Seeker: "Tell me, father."

Abbot: "Of course not, son. Free will is man's natural walking stick. Because he can choose to love; he may also be hateful. And because he can choose to be good; he may also be evil. It is so. Man must choose and he must choose well. Ah, beware of the temptress my son, beware!"

Seeker: "Who is the temptress, father?"

Abbot: "Only the holy spirit of mind can lead and protect man on the path of righteousness. The temptress also resides in his mind, it is the egoistic mind; alas, it is the ego and its objects my son, beware!"

Seeker: "Father, if the ego can trample and override man's freewill which ought to be directed by the holy spirit of the mind, then the ego must be domineering indeed."

Abbot: "Son, the soul is willing but the body is weak."

Seeker: "Father, some people vehemently argue against free will and maintain that man's actions are predetermined. They say man is helplessly obsequious to fate and that like a puppet, his strings are toyed with by a power greater than him. How does this compare with what you've just said about free will?"

Abbot: "They are hypocrites, who would rather shirk the responsibility of their freewill and hope to steer clear of accountability. But alas, hypocrites are merely afraid; they fear to wield the power of freedom. The freedom to choose to do good despite the pleasures of evil. The freedom to love unconditionally in a world dying of hate. The freedom of completeness and limitlessness for some is too bewildering and overwhelming; therefore, cannot be real. Son, freedom is the ultimate virtue and man is not without it by nature."

Seeker: "Father, what about political and economic freedoms? Are people not attracted to do evil because of some economic returns or to be hateful because of some political differences? For there are many external variables that encroach on man's freedom to be himself."

Abbot: "Son, man's economic and political freedoms are only possible when the collective destiny of man is achieved through cooperation and unity. The prevalence of religious persecutions; political sufferance; social differences; and the age-old canker of poverty are but the loud symptoms of your divisions, among a lot more silent things that foment the foregoing.

If a man denies his religious divisions, would he endure persecution? If a man denies his political divisions, would he suffer the agony of ideology? If a man denies his racism, would he be pained by envy and jealousy? If one shares his loaf of bread, would his brother go hungry?"

Seeker: "Indeed not, father. Please tell me more about economic and political freedoms."

Abbot: "Son, freedom is not attainable through external factors. It lives in the inner sanctuary of the man himself, and until he can find it in himself and wield his inner light with faith, his attempts to seek freedom externally would only bring him pains and chains. Man seeks economic freedom to amass wealth, and to pleasure himself with the numerous bizarre artifacts and entertainments of his civilization. The lack of which brings him pains; the fulfillment of which brings him chains. If he were wiser than he pretends to be, wouldn't he dispense with his pains and chains?"

Seeker: "Indeed, father."

Abbot: "Man upholds one ideology and castigates the other, all the while fomenting trouble; and then turns around to bemoan the whips and taxes of his tyrants. His society honors and gives status to its tyrants, and sings praise songs after them. His history books eulogize and immortalize tyrants, and make mockery out of their misdeeds. Son, is man not the maker of tyrants?"

Seeker: "He is indeed the maker of tyrants, father. What about prisoners?"

Abbot: "Your societies honor tyrants and imprison criminals; both of whom are created by the self-same society with its patronage and vilification. Has man asked himself what makes the tyrant tyrannical and what makes the prisoner criminal? If you disrobe the tyrant of his titles, prestige, and alas, his ego, what you have left is a simple human being who had been misled by his society. If you dismantle the prison walls and disabuse the criminal of his greed, covetousness, and alas, his ego, what you have left is a simple human being who had been misled by his society.

Both the tyrant and the criminal are creatures of their society; for no man was born a tyrant nor a criminal. Do you see then, son, that to be free from tyranny and crime, man must be free of the ego, the temptress?"

Seeker: "Indeed, father, it is as you say. What about slaves? Many are the captives whose hands and feet and necks are shackled with tight iron chains; and sold and bought as chattel. Father, this inhumane practice is as old as mankind and has been justified in one way or the other by slavers and slaves alike. What do you make of this assassination of freedom?"

Abbot: "Son, man is free to choose. Because he can choose to be kind and compassionate to his fellow man; he may also choose to be mean and wicked to him. Because he can choose to give charity and property to his fellow man; he may also choose to seize and make property out of him. Because he can choose to be hardworking and work the field himself; he may also choose to be indolent and use the labors of others. Because he can choose to be peaceful and neighborly towards his fellow; he may also choose the path of aggression and discord. And because he can choose to be righteous and loving; his ego may tempt him to choose sin and corruption. And because he allows his ego to tempt him, he could invent a thousand justifications for what he does. But is he justified?"

Seeker: "Indeed not, father."

Abbot: "Son, from our blissful repose, we have seen many epochs and generations of mankind come and go. We have seen slavers become slaves and we have equally seen slaves become slavers. We have seen the painful tears of slaves lose their bitterness and become joyful tears and we have equally seen the joyful tears of slavers become painful tears. We have seen slaves break free from their captivity and become kings and we have equally seen kings become bitter and sore slaves. We have seen merchant ships become slave ships and we have equally seen slave ships become merchant ships. We have seen slave chains melted and turned into trinkets and we have equally seen trinkets melted and turned into slave chains. If man were wiser than he pretends to be, surely, he would choose that which is permanent and enduring than the crops and trinkets made with slave labor."

Seeker: "Indeed father, you have seen a lot. Please tell me, can man enslave his fellows in the name of achieving higher purposes for society?"

Abbot: "Son, look at the rubbles and remnants of the great castles and city walls of antiquity till now and tell me, what higher purposes do you see amongst them? Look at the unmarked graves of all the slaves who died on battlefields and cotton fields and tell me, what higher purposes do you see? Imagine all the pains and suffering of all the slaves and slavers alike and tell me, what higher purposes do you see? Imagine all the unrealized potentialities and unused geniuses of all those who were trapped in chains and tell me, what higher purposes were being achieved?

Seeker: "Indeed none, father."

Abbot: "The highest purpose that should be strived for is the achievement of the collective destiny of man through cooperation and unity. But he cannot cooperate and unite with his fellows if he is not self-realized and therefore capable of unconditional love.

Who, being self-realized and compassionate, would enchain and brutalize his fellow, even for all the wealth in the world? Who, being self-realized and intelligent, would fiendishly exact the labor of his fellow without their consent? Who, being self-realized and joyful, would deny his fellow the opportunity to enjoy life happily without the indignity of enslavement? Son, only self-knowledge and love can lead man to cooperate and unite; and only cooperation and unity will solve all of man's problems."

Seeker: "Father, are men driven to enslave others because of the scarcity of resources and their need for survival? For what would cause a merchant ship to become a slave ship?"

Abbot: "Indeed son, the Earth spins through times and seasons. There are times when the clouds hide their blessings and the land is hard and crops do not fare well. There are also times of pestilence and other hardships that bring famine and hunger to man. There are times when wicked men reign over your countries and cause havoc to the livelihoods of their subjects. There are indeed times of scarcity of resources and man rises against his fellow man to dominate him and appropriate his resources. There are indeed times of scarcity when merchants lose profits for want of merchandise and might resort to slavery. There are equally times when man's need for survival makes him vulnerable and drives him straight into the gaping mouth of treachery and slavery.

The Earth indeed spins through times and seasons but what is permanent through all this, is man himself; the strong arms and hands of Existence; the quick legs and feet of Existence; the brilliance of the intellect of Existence; the love of the intelligence of Existence; the kindness of the compassion of Existence. Son, hard times are not meant to condemn man to brutishness but to awaken him to himself and to bring out his best.

The scarcity of resources is an opportunity to share and appreciate that which is taken for granted. Scarcity should incense and lead man into the exploration of that which he hadn't imagined. Alas, when scarcity drives man into survival then he misses the point and he becomes bitter and brutish; seizing and pillaging; vandalizing humanity for avarice and power, the reason why he enslaves."

Seeker: "Indeed, father. What is the worst form of slavery?"

Abbot: "Son, man's body may be enslaved and every bit of strength squeezed out of him, but a far more insidious crime against man is the enslavement of his mind. In this regard, many slaves are not enchained but gallivant freely in the streets and sleep comfortably in their homes. For their chains and fetters are their ignorance and gullibility; their gluttony and lustfulness; their fears and conformities. And alas, their slavers are truth-mufflers and whisperers, scriptures and doctrines, sects, and their dogmas. For these seek to divide, conquer, and rule the minds of men and indeed, subvert the destiny of mankind, which is in working together with love."

Seeker: "I am enlivened by your words, father, such poignancy. How does an enslaved mind work?"

Abbot: "Like fishes of shallow waters; they flip and flap themselves with delight and pleasure themselves in the warmth of warmer waters, easier depths. Their gluttony and lustfulness stray them into the fisherman's net and self-realization is only achieved when it is too late. Like stray dogs, they abandon the solemnity of their father's house and seek profligacy in dirty streets and amusement parks. Self-realization comes to them only too late when they hear whistling and the screeching sound of knife-sharpening.

Like moons that receive light but would not share theirs; they shirk their duty and cower in their ignorance. For the power to wield freedom from ignorance and gullibility; freedom from lust and amusement; and freedom to do their duty is already theirs. It is rooted in deep waters and resides in their father's house, the inner sanctuary. Ah, the comforts of ignorance my son."

Seeker: "Father, what about the sincerity of the many people who follow one sect or the other; with the hope and faith of pleasing their God and doing what is right? Surely, all these people cannot have gone astray as you have said."

Abbot: "Son, underneath their sincerity, is a prayer for special favors over others, underneath their sincerity is a desire for Heaven, and underneath their sincerity is venom against other sects, other humans, whom they call heathens. Their hope for the betterment of their Lot is also the silent hope for the dissipation of the Lot of others. In their faith in their God, is also the murder of the God of others. Son, sincerity, hope, and faith exercised in ignorance have no meaning whatsoever and only give furtherance to man's divisions and suffering.

And being sincerely astray is still being astray. The pain of ignorance is that; its antidote is already in man's grip. Man cannot shirk his duty of self-knowledge and love, for how would he contribute to the collective good and unity of the world?"

Seeker: "So no mercy for the ignorant?"

Abbot: "Absolutely none, son. Man needs no pity, for he is complete and wholesome, and only needs to disabuse himself of that which leads him astray, the temptress. For it is the ego that covets Heaven; it is the ego that condemns others and delights in its illusive superiority and indeed, son, the ego is a bundle of ignorance."

Seeker: "So what becomes of such people, the lot of mankind?"

Abbot: "Retreat, draw inwardly, back to their father's house, and be diligent in stillness for grace to find them there. For man left his father's house and now having seen the light of truth and turning back, he ought to save his society by glowing with love. Man must not choose the path of being care-free my son because it is sad for such a precious thing as human life to be wasted in ignorance my son."

Seeker: "What about future generations?"

Abbot: "The future is a potentiality with innumerable possibilities my son. If man doesn't change today, the future remains the same. What happens today is what determines what will happen tomorrow, and today is joyfully responsive to man's actions. Man's salvation is in his firm grip and surely, the age of ignorance and deception shall slack into oblivion when the sons of man shall turn their backs on the torch of truth-mufflers and weasels.

Glorious are the future generations of mankind when men shall be self-realized and love effortlessly and unconditionally. Glorious are the future generations when man shall be his torchbearer. Joyous are the days ahead when man shall look back and celebrate what barbarity he had jettisoned. And truth shall prevail, and the forces of darkness shall succumb to light. Harken to my words oh son."

Seeker: "So man's hope is in his future generations?"

Abbot: "Son, hope is a hoax; it has no reality but is loaded with man's fears and wishes. The future is a potentiality and like all potentialities, what you do to achieve it is crucial to its materialization. Man cannot sit on the fence and merely hope, he'll achieve nothing and the machinery of the grand deception shall keep rolling. Only man himself can break the wheel of deception with his love-directed action and neighborliness; for one bad nut may yet corrupt the whole."

Seeker: "Can self-realized people be corrupted?"

Abbot: "No, son. But the presence of one bad nut makes the whole unwholesome. Until there's no division, the whole is not."

Seeker: "Father, will this not take forever to achieve since all people must individually change?"

Abbot: "Son, time is irrelevant in eternity and to that which is eternal. If four cornerstones can start a new building then surely, a dozen-dozen thousand men may yet regenerate a new generation of mankind. The roots of ignorance and deception may yet survive mild winds but strong winds leave no stone unturned and reveal what had been suppressed by ignorance and deception. Harken to my words oh son."

Seeker: "Are the current actions and efforts of man like mild winds?"

Abbot: "Yes, son. But winds do gather momentum and strength and may yet uproot a mighty decaying tree."

Seeker: "So the joyous future is inevitable?"

Abbot: "Absolutely and definitely."

Seeker: "Even without man's actions, deliberate or otherwise?"

Abbot: "To be a man is to act, and the ego cannot delay man from doing his duty any more than the eclipse can hide the Sun from doing its duty. All actions shall converge at the threshold of truth sooner or later; for the wrong doer is a mirror to the righteous and the righteous, a model to the wrong doer. In the end, the truth shall prevail; the wrong doer shall see what pettiness he had made of his life and turn over a new leaf."

Seeker: "Father, won't there be judgment and condemnation for the wrong doer?"

Abbot: "Truth only longs to be truthful; not to judge nor condemn. Ah, the eternity of truth my son."

Seeker: "So a person will not suffer any consequences for sinning, even if ignorantly?"

Abbot: "Son, only the ignorant sins and all sins stem from the ego. And sin contains all the punishment it deserves. If one acts in ignorance and suffers in ignorance; what consequences shall truth seek? Look at the heavy chains of greediness and covetousness and look at the pains of mischievousness and lustfulness, and tell me what consequences should be suffered. Imagine the agony of realizing that one had led a false life, an egocentric life, and tell me, son, what consequences shall truth seek that are weightier than what the ego had wrought?"

Seeker: "What about murder, shouldn't man suffer any punishment for taking the life of another?"

Abbot: "Murder is evil and people with evil tendencies should be sequestered and cared for. And caring means loving. They should be loved and reformed, for in them are many great potentials. It has been said by your scriptures and laws that justice demands an eye for an eye and a life for a life but son, it is never just to take life or maim as punishment for that which was wrought in ignorance. Only love would understand this. If it is punishment in the afterlife that you're asking about then know this, son, the soul does not bear the guilt of the false self. The soul is faultless, unblemished, and innocent; now and always. And when the sins and evils of the gross ego are cast down together with the body in the moment of death, man is relieved of all guilt and condemnation.

But son, it is man's society that suffers and it suffers its creations. Is your society not the maker of egos?"

Seeker: "Indeed, father, it is."

Abbot: "Your religions promote sin and evil when they assure man that his sins would be forgiven if only, he would ask God for forgiveness or if he would pay tithes and buy indulgences. Your cultures reduce men to children and tell them sweet things that sway them to sin and evil. It is man's society that is guilty of all the murders and evils on Earth my son."

Seeker: "Father, can self-realized men use their gained wisdom and inner light to influence society and others, to benefit from it? Would it ever be possible for a soul-centered person to go back to their egocentric tendencies and do things that may be considered sinful by other self-realized people?"

Abbot: "Son, firstly, wisdom and inner light are not gained but rather are uncovered from the veil of the ego. Men have said to one another that 'in the land of the blind, the one-eyed man is a king' and this is true both literally and figuratively. But son, added to the one-eyed man of self-realization are the powers of love which forbid sinning and is the most-dependable compass of the soul that I told you of.

However, son, men who operate at the level of the soul are also cognizant of the weakness of the body and its vulnerability and susceptibility to the ego; therefore, they subject themselves to and are guided by self-recognized and self-imposed laws of their own volition, as opposed to being proscribed by external authority. These laws for such men become part and parcel of their sense of truth, the violating of which brings to them a debilitating sense of betrayal of their souls and therefore God, the Divine, and all that is true.

Son, truly self-realized people seek unity and collective progress for mankind and therefore make their endeavors in the world instrumental for societal growth. Who and what they influence with their love-directed actions must as a matter of course be beneficial to society. But if they are found wanting, then, son, they were never self-realized. Many self-deluded men tout themselves about as all manner of persons, bearing decorated titles, and they are known by the coin they collect."

Seeker: "Father, but why should the Divine or the one God allow clever or self-deluded people to wield so much influence?"

Abbot: "Son, the Great Circle gives abundantly and equally to its creations. It cannot therefore interfere in the affairs and relationships of men because it gives all men free will. To each man, it gave all the powers a man can have. To each man it blessed with all the gifts of the Earth. To each man, it gave utility to the holy spirit of the mind. And to each man, it gave eyes and ears, and legs and arms. Free will and indeed, freedom is the pinnacle of the love the Divine has for man and men must wield it autonomously and wisely, son. The soul that sins is the soul that follows another's instruction and worships their influence. Seek not to influence others and no matter what, never be influenced by another; not by their words, their actions, their flamboyance, their modesty, their possessions and what have you."

Seeker: "Indeed, father. But why hasn't mankind changed up to now?"

Abbot: "Again son, time is irrelevant to eternity and to that which is eternal. Mankind is always changing and ever nearer to his maker, to himself; which he is estranged unto. But remember, until the last bad nut turns over a new leaf, the whole is not. Son, man's progress cannot be measured in time for that which he progresses towards lives in timelessness, it is ever nearer in him, it is here, it is now. Your epoch may look back at far-gone generations of mankind and measure your progress in time, by the millennia and what have you, but that which lived then is the self-same thing that lives now in you, son. Again, time and impermanence have no substance to that which is eternal; and man's maker is ever present, ever nearer in him."

Seeker: "Father, what is time?"

Abbot: "Son, time is a tricky and complex thing but I will try to make it simple. Think of time as a measure of movements; from one point to another and from one event to another. It can be any movement; for instance, the movement between two blinks, the movement between two breaths, the movement between two echoes, the movement between two heartbeats, etc. It can also be the movement of thinking, the movement of blood through the veins, the movement of the limbs, the movement of the lips, etc.

It is also cosmic movement; for instance, the movement or rotation of Earth on its axis, the movement or revolution of the planets around the Sun, the movement of your solar system amidst other systems, the movement of your galaxy, and so forth.

It is also a small movement; for instance, the movement of hydrogen into helium, the movement of electrons around the nucleus of an atom, the movement of cell division, and more.

In a nutshell, son, that which has time has movement and that which has movement has time."

Seeker: "Indeed, father."

Abbot: "Son, also think of time as two-fold; intrinsic time and extrinsic time. Intrinsic time is further composed of two forms, that is intrinsic somatic time and intrinsic psychological time. Intrinsic somatic time is those biological and physiological movements that are necessary for life, for example, breathing, blood flowing, heart beating, etc. which depend on the body's circadian rhythms to function properly. In old age, these movements reduce leading to a reduction in the vibrancy of the biological time or intrinsic somatic time of the person. A child does have more intrinsic somatic time than a grown man just as a healthy person has more of it than a sick person. Intrinsic somatic time is relative to each person.

Intrinsic psychological time on the other hand has two types; personal Intrinsic psychological time and universal intrinsic psychological time. Personal Intrinsic psychological time refers to time as it relates personally to an individual conscious observer in a localized plane, such as on Earth. It is time as recognizable by the conscious observer, comprising their earliest memories to the present and until their death. Personal intrinsic psychological time is relative and subjective to each conscious observer.

Universal intrinsic psychological time is time measured in common or objectively by the given population of a world of multiple conscious observers, such as is the case on Earth. And so, the collective memories and histories of mankind occur chronologically, as measured as universal Intrinsic psychological time. Son, this is where all your great heroes, great deeds, great ideas, great religions, great militaries and what have you, reside in time. A great time indeed; divided into millennia, centuries, and decades. Universal intrinsic psychological time is objective but may not always be the case. Someone's universal intrinsic psychological time may be limited to their small country or community, their personal intrinsic psychological time, and a few others whereas another person's perception of universal intrinsic psychological time could span millennia and vast distances. And like all the other forms of time, universal Intrinsic psychological time also has a beginning, a span, and an end.

Both intrinsic somatic time and personal Intrinsic psychological time come to an end in the death of the body and ego respectively of an individual conscious observer. Upon the conception of the child, movements begin in the zygote, and time is occasioned, and upon the conception of the man, movements begin in his egoistic mind, and time is occasioned. Whereas the death of the individual would end personal Intrinsic psychological time and intrinsic somatic time, it does not bring an end to universal intrinsic psychological time. However long, universal intrinsic psychological time also comes to an end when an epoch dies and many have died."

Seeker: "Indeed, father. So, intrinsic time is time that is measured from the perspective of conscious observers like men on Earth? And intrinsic somatic time, personal Intrinsic psychological time, and universal intrinsic psychological time are all subject to a beginning, a span, and an end?"

Abbot: "Correct, son."

Seeker: "What about extrinsic time?"

Abbot: "Extrinsic time relates to movements of cosmic bodies. These movements occur with or without a conscious observer to measure and delineate them. For instance, the movement of Earth on its axis and around the Sun occasions time which Earthlings can measure, divide, and count; likewise, the movement of Neptune also occasions time but without conscious observers to measure from the localized perspective of Neptune.

Son, you may also think of extrinsic time as two types; localized extrinsic time and unlocalized extrinsic time. Localized extrinsic time is time generated by the movement of a cosmic body that is subjected and subservient to a larger cosmic body in a localized system such as the movement of Earth and the other planets around the Sun. In localized extrinsic time, there's always a constant point of reference for the subservient moving bodies to delineate a time interval or duration. If the Earth revolved around a dark object and therefore didn't receive the Sun's beacon; day and night could not be separated and neither could the years be counted. Do you follow, son?"

Seeker: "Indeed, father, every word."

Abbot: "Also, localized extrinsic time is not always the same for all the planetary bodies of a star. Each planet generates its own localized extrinsic time based on its speed and the nature of its movement. Earth has a different and smaller localized extrinsic time than Neptune because it is closer to the Sun and therefore revolves around it at a shorter orbit than Neptune does. Earthlings would have counted one-hundred and sixty-five years of revolutions around the Sun before a Neptunian revolution was complete. Similarly, Mercury, though closer to the Sun and makes a complete revolution in eighty-eight Earth days, rotates very slowly on its axis therefore its daytime is as long as fifty-nine Earth days. So, son, if all the planets were populated with conscious observers, you can imagine how difficult it could have been to keep track of all the differences and nuances of the movements of celestial bodies, even in one solar system."

Seeker: "Indeed, father. I see that time as per localized extrinsic time is one that is characterized by the fixed revolution or movement of a planet around its central star, and that is called a Year. And, by movement or rotation of a planet on its axis; the part of the planet facing the Sun we call Day, and the part facing away from the Sun, we call Night. Also, localized extrinsic time does not always require the presence of a conscious observer to occur. Am I correct, father?"

Abbot: "Yes, absolutely correct, son. Neptune makes its revolutions whether someone is there to count them as years or not, and Mercury sluggishly rotates on its axis whether someone is there to count its days and nights."

Seeker: "Indeed, father. What about unlocalized extrinsic time?"

Abbot: "Unlocalized extrinsic time is time as generated by cosmic bodies that do not have a constant or fixed point of reference; like interstellar objects and galaxies. Such objects generate only intrinsic time, as relating to their parts, and cannot generate extrinsic time because they are not bound to a fixed point of reference, like a star."

Seeker: "Father, how is man making progress towards Oneness, what has changed in time?"

Abbot: "The eclipse of the light of love is passing with alacrity and the heavens nod in agreement and with excitement. The stars are ever closer to Earth and the winds are gathering momentum and strength. False gods and other instruments of your divisions are fleeing the scene with cast-down faces. The leeches and fleas that feast on man's wounds have been scorched to death and he heals from their infestations. Man has jumped off the backs of truth-mufflers and weasels and is making steady steps on his own to that which he owns by right. But alas, not all is well, son. The ego festers in ignorance and many are led astray; undoing the collective good and unity of man."

Seeker: "What are the interests of truth-mufflers and weasels? Are they servants of darkness? For if they are bent on subverting man's destiny, surely there must be some reasons why they would not want man's destiny realized, Father."

Abbot: "Indeed, son. It is as you say, the wealthy and powerful delight themselves very much in your divisions; and they would do what they must to keep you divided and ignorant. Truth is light and ignorance is darkness; and so yes, they are servants of darkness. It is in the darkness that their status and prestige mean something. It is in darkness that men are afraid. It is in darkness that men conform and follow like a herd. It is in darkness that men are led astray. It is in darkness that wrongdoers subsist. Son, they are indeed servants of darkness.

And while they serve darkness for their parochial interests and amusement; it is truth that shall have the last laugh. When the supremacy of death visits them in their last moments and their castles and estates appear to them like chaff, they shall then know that it is the truth that has had the last laugh."

Seeker: "But father, while they are living and enjoying their status and wealth, it is they who are laughing at the collective destiny of man and delaying the inevitable demise of darkness. What can man do to spite the ignorant and achieve its destiny of cooperation and unity?"

Abbot: "Again son, deny your divisions; until the last bad nut is not. Disrobe your cassocks and untie your turbans. Disdain from your primitive rituals and abandon your grotesque temples of stone and gold. Deny your divisions; until the last false god is not. Un-read your scriptures and unwind the loops of traditions. Unburden your hearts and minds from dogmatism and flee from its sharp-knife of division. Alas, son, deny your divisions; until the last medium is suffocated of homage and patronage. Distance yourself from all dogmatic claimants of the Divine; for it cannot be divvied up.

But to do all this, man must see for himself that it is so. Man must first retreat inwardly to find his light and be his torchbearer. Man must enshrine himself in the inner temple and bind with the Divine; bring himself to the directionless stillness of the Divine and see for himself the Oneness that engulfs all and sundry. Man's circle must be impervious to the allure of the ego and its objects. Man must no longer cower and take shelter in naïve sincerity that conforms to the instruments of his divisions but be the strong arm of the Divine and assert himself for the collective destiny of mankind. He must be the arrow head of truth that pierces the bubble of ignorance and blows away the darkness that surrounds him. Harken to my words oh son."

Seeker: "Indeed, father. But man appears to prefer to believe in dogmas and gods, and be defensive in his beliefs. What will wake man up from the illusion of belief?"

Abbot: "Son, man doesn't only prefer the illusion of belief; he is impulsive to it. Man is born into a culture of believing right from his parentage and he grows up with it. It weaves into him so deeply; that it becomes second nature. It is forged into his ego and his personality so immensely; that he feels it necessary to assert and defend it. The glue of indoctrination is so sticky that only a few men can unstick themselves from it. The prison of the illusion of belief is so comfortable that man locks himself in, swallows the key, digests it into his bloodstream, and passes his beliefs down his bloodline to continue the opiate stream of believing. Ah, the comforts of belief my son."

Seeker: "Indeed, father. But man is enjoined to follow in the footsteps of his parents, to love and respect them unquestionably. How can the sons of man unstick themselves from the stickiness of their parental and traditional indoctrination?"

Abbot: "Son, every soul is accountable for itself and man is his soul, not his body. Your parents and ancestry are the source and pride of your body but your soul is its circle; complete, wholesome, and eternal. Your parents and your children are your companions in the Divine and you must indeed love and respect each other. When self-inquiry and knowledge lead you to see for yourself that you are in a prison of illusions; it is your Divine duty to regurgitate the key and free yourself to establish a new bloodline. For it is inhumane and insane to continue with falsities after the veil of illusion has been cast down. Ah, the sobriety of the opiate stream my son."

Seeker: "Indeed, father. But often, deviating from the stream leads to mean rejection; insults, and harm; and alas, sometimes what is called honor killing. This engenders the comfort of toeing the line of tradition and conforming to the community. Should a man suffer the brutalities of deviating and living the truth?"

Abbot: "Truth cannot be rejected by illusion; it is the other way around. Truth cannot be insulted or harmed by illusion; it is the other way around. And certainly, truth cannot be killed by illusion; it is the other way around. Son, it is the lack of courage that makes men suffer because of being rejected, insulted, or harmed by folks who revel in their illusions. And when one dies for upholding the truth; he loses only his body for his soul shall live to proclaim the truth another day. Ah, the joy of eternity my son."

Seeker: "Father, what about the other comforts of belief? Does man himself not derive a sense of security and pleasure from his beliefs?"

Abbot: "Indeed he does, son. Alas, it is his ego that shelters in beliefs, and pleasures itself with the illusory artifacts of ideas, hopes, and wishes. But what man is, is eternal, complete, and wholesome which doesn't need a sense of security; it drools with everlasting bliss."

Seeker: "Would you not be tearing a man apart when you take his beliefs away?"

Abbot: "No, you'd be tearing his ego apart. And who shall mourn for the death of the ego my son? But, no one can take away man's beliefs. If someone else convinces a man to abandon a belief, he might replace it with another belief and no belief is sacrosanct. Only man can see for himself the falsity of belief and once seen, the act of believing would be relegated to mundane affairs. And belief would no longer have a place in the holy sphere of the Divine."

Seeker: "Are blessed they who believe even without seeing? What is the nature of belief, father?"

Abbot: "Son, words are grandly limited when it comes to understanding or referencing the Divine. Belief as a word cannot be used about that which is unknowable. For you cannot make an estimation of that which is immeasurable. You may believe in something based on inference or estimation, in which case, you're guessing or hoping that something is the case. But you cannot guess or hope about the Divine. Man cannot believe or disbelieve the Divine because he has no inference or estimation for it. He may believe or disbelieve in the gods of his cultures and his creation but the Divine is beyond measurement.

When man sees for himself in the hallowed dome of his inner sanctuary his Oneness with the Divine; he'll not speak of belief, and alas, he'll not guess nor hope. For blessed are they who see and know."

Seeker: "Indeed, father. What about faith? It is said that those with a strong faith can do anything to prove it, including sacrificing their lives or that of their loved ones. What is faith?"

Abbot: "Son, faith is one of the strands of the beam of the light of love, man's essence, as I have already told you. It is a refined form of passion and is unleashed because of man's diligent pursuit of the inner realm. It is a sign of self-knowledge and brightens man's aura with the profuseness of the Divine. Faith emboldens the heart of a self-realized man and strengthens his spirit of mind to be a trailblazer in the name of the Divine. Love is faithful and faith nurtures and loves. Son, faith doesn't need proving; neither to the one God nor to oneself. A self-realized man is naturally effulgent with faith; for it is in his love and nature to be faithful."

Seeker: "Indeed, father. Are there different kinds of faith?"

Abbot: "No, son. But there is something called blind faith, which requires testing and proving; for it is exercised in ignorance. It is an exaggerated form of belief for it is based on hope and wishes; hollowness. Indeed, son, blind faith is zealous, extremist, and obsequious naivete; seeking to please its object of worship. Beware of zealots, extremists, and hypocrites who tout the name of the Divine for their intentions, beware!"

Seeker: "Father, what about blind faith exercised in sincerity and innocence?"

Abbot: "It is still blind faith and ignorance, son. Man must embark on the journey himself which he is already equipped for; he must climb the mountain to its summit and see for himself. To sincerely have faith in what others who have climbed and have seen and have said has no meaning or substance in the grand scheme of the Great Circle. Ah, the hollowness of mediocrity and followership."

Seeker: "What roles do belief and blind faith play in the divisions of man?"

Abbot: "Son, are belief and blind faith not the instruments of your religious divisions and contentions? Are your religious bigotry and zealotry not the causes of your so-called holy wars and persecutions? Are your national borders not drawn based on your religions? Are your heavens and hells not separated based on your religions? Are your laws and scriptures not different and decreed by your religions? Are your holy places not separated by your sectarian religious claims? Are your sins and taboos not proscribed by the instructions of your religions? Son, man is sorely divided because he believes in different gods and blindly follows different sects; which are but the creatures of his cultures."

Seeker: "Father, but the world is huge and has different races of people who have developed different cultures over millennia of societal growth. Surely, their religions, which are ways to commune with the Divine, would also be different and would reflect the obvious cultural differences that had ensued, is that not so?"

Abbot: "Correct son, it is as you say. Indeed, there have been numerous cultural explosions and epochs, in man's journey from the caves and valleys to your present times. And still, man retains his cultural differences and asserts his dogmatic and exclusive claims on the indivisible Oneness of the Divine; leading to alienation and discord between the races of men. Your cultures create and idealize different gods and heavens. Your cultures honor different holy places and rituals. Your cultures uphold different laws and proscribe different sins. Your cultures cut through the unity and equality of man like razors and set man against man; hailing one as holy and the other, as heathen. Son, is culture not the very source of your divisions?"

Seeker: "Indeed, father. Is the Oneness of the Divine beyond question?"

Abbot: "Yes, beyond question my son. If there are multiple, then there are multiple existences and multiple creations but that is an absurd thought, much less factual. There is only Oneness, son."

Seeker: "Father, does the Oneness have a name? I ask because every culture has a name for the one God which they insist is the real and actual name of the one God. They invoke it in prayers and persecutions. They inscribe it on their war banners and breathe it out when throwing their spears at the enemy. They chant it in their victory songs and cry it out in times of sorrow. Can the same Oneness have different names?"

Abbot: "Indeed not, son. Speech is based on language and words are the instruments of your languages; and because man must move from silence and speak, he creates a language. Man's languages do not function well without the act of naming things for references, and so, he names everything including the un-namable. He gives the Divine a name, a gender, and other human characteristics. Once a thing is named, it begins to develop a character and amasses attributes over time. This character and its loaded attributes are assigned by man himself despite what he might want to believe.

Son, from our blissful repose, we have seen many cultures arise from oblivion, expand, and collapse into oblivion. They all assign the Divine names with a myriad of arcane origins but as their cultures tumble, so do the names. Son, the Divine is eternal, beyond time; and that which is eternal cannot be named by a culture that arises and dies, nor in a language that is subject to time. But alas, man must do what he does; naming things.

Man personifies the Divine and leads himself on through his very capable imagination to believe that because the Divine has a personhood, and while forgetting his role in that personification; He must equally want some things and hate others, as men do. That the Divine must have a home in the heavens; that He must have a consort and children; that He must have a throne from which He gives commandments; that He must have servant angels and principalities; that He must have nepotism and love sycophancy; and alas, that He must have an enemy, whom they have equally named Devil."

Seeker: "Father, you said a man is eternal and that which is eternal cannot be named; yet men have names. What do you say about that?"

Abbot: "Son, it is man's soul that is complete, wholesome, and eternal; his circle. However, when he is born into his culture, the dictates of his culture give him a name. His name is tied to his body and dies with his body; his soul, the 'I', has no name for it is eternal, beyond any language and culture. If you must name a thing that is eternal and universal, which of your innumerable languages and cultures would have the singular privilege to do the honors?"

Seeker: "Indeed, Father, it cannot be so; for each tongue has a name for it."

Abbot: "Correct, son. Its name is innumerable, infinite, and unfathomable."

Seeker: "Father, am I to understand from your previous statements that he whom man had given the name Devil and personified as the arch enemy of the Divine is a figment of man's imagination?"

Abbot: "Indeed, son. Man uses his intellect to pierce through the Oneness of the Divine in his attempt to answer his questions about the world; amidst confusion, wonderment, and fear. The intellect uses two processes of analysis to derive its conclusions; thinking and ideating. He thinks based on memories, realities, and motives; and he ideates based on idealisms, imaginations, and of course, motives. In both cases he desires what he had already conceived and emoted, even before his analysis; so, the thinking and ideating are a way to find plausible explanations for his motives which must inevitably stem from his ego and its conditioning.

But son, as I have already told you, memory is limited in time and can be erroneous. Secondly, man fancies idealisms that respond positively to his desires and wishes. The products of thinking are thoughts and the products of ideating are ideas; both of which are grandly limited in time and therefore cannot answer questions about timelessness or oneness. But he continues in this exercise of futility and fantasy of the ego, which wants to measure and posit conclusions in names, words, and verses.

To measure is to move from two feet to nine feet, and to move from the Earth to the moon. To measure is to move from yesterday to today, and to move from today to tomorrow. To measure is to move from the past to the present; and to move from the present to the future. To measure is to move from day to night; and to move from light to darkness. To measure is to move from cold to hot, and to move from liquid to vapor. To measure is to move from love to hate; and to move from like to dislike. To measure is to move from unity to division; and to move from cooperation to discord. To measure is to move from good to evil; and to move from the Divine to the Devil. And alas, son, to measure is to move from Oneness to duality, to separation, to lies."

Seeker: "Indeed, father. But the Devil stands almost as tall as the Divine in the lives and thinking of many people on Earth. He is believed to be the bringer of doom and the whisperer of evil to man. He is believed to seduce men to sin and strays their feet from righteousness. These beliefs are deeply rooted in man and are the source of many fears. Father, is the Devil a lie?"

Abbot: "Son, the Devil is indeed a lie. It is the composite of man's fears and unfaithfulness. It is a caricature of his creation to take the fall for his misdeeds. Man, calling out the Devil is like a dog barking at its reflection in a mirror but as you know son, the reflection is but a mirage and has no substance to it. But how can you convince the dog that its reflection is only a mirage of itself? It is not within the composure of a self-realized man to accommodate such thinking and beliefs, much less the existence of such an entity. How contemptuous and blasphemous is the mind that nurtures and fears the Devil? How dare he, the man who conjures an enemy for the Divine? Son, there is only Oneness."

Seeker: "Indeed, father. It is scriptural postulations that lead man to accept the Devil as a reality. The story goes that in the beginning, there was a big fight in Heaven where the Devil rebelled against God, leading to his banishment to Earth. Apart from the story, man also sees around him that great evil exists and cannot be from God, who is good and therefore the Devil must exist as a tormentor of God's creation. What do you have to say about this, father?"

Abbot: "Son, you are right, man is beleaguered with enormous reasons and pressures to believe in the Devil. But alas, only the ignorant believe; self-realized people know for sure. It is not a story but a mythical depiction of man's cosmology, among many other myths and cosmologies we have witnessed from our blissful repose over millennia. If you believe in something and if you want something to be true regardless of its veracity, then mythologies are very potent tools for convincing would-be believers. But alas, mythologies are the products of man's very capable imagination and have no substance in them.

Long ago when man was still very young and primitive, afraid and bewildered; wise men created mythologies to calm their nerves and enable them to cope with the wonderment and treachery that surrounded them. Now man believes in myths as true stories and the wise men who created them have had amnesia. So, the grand deception keeps festering and man is none the wiser.

Son, only self-knowledge can release man from the claws of mythology and illusion. Nobody and no books can tell you what Heaven looks like or what happens there; only the holy gate of death shall reveal the afterlife. Ah, the holy gate of death my son."

Seeker: "Indeed father. What about the reality of great evil that pertains on Earth, leading man to believe that it must come from a great evil power like the Devil?"

Abbot: "Harken to my words oh son; there's only Oneness and man is part and parcel of his oneness with the Divine. Man is his soul and his soul doesn't know separation nor measurement. It doesn't know Evil from Good, nor the Devil from Divine. It doesn't know anything outside Oneness for there's no outsideness to Oneness. What measures, evaluates, judges, and condemns, is the false self, the ego; which is a conditioned entity. That which is conditioned is conditioned with certain attributes, such as likes and dislikes, moral and immoral, good and evil, us and them, etc. Son, the false self, or the ego is the true nemesis of Oneness, and it is a creation of man's societies and their cultures.

As you know, son, what is liked in one culture may be disliked in another. And what is morally reprehensible in one culture may be morally praiseworthy in another. And what is considered by one society as good may be considered as evil in another society. And one man's God could be another man's Devil. It is all the works and shenanigans of the false self and reflects its society. But the true self, the soul, knows only Oneness and its essential nature is love, bliss.

Indeed, son, there's great evil in the world caused by none other but the false self. Remember, only the ignorant sin and sinning, is evil. Son, mention one evil deed that cannot be traced to the false self, the ego?"

Seeker: "Would you consider murder as evil? I ask because many people believe so, and believe it is the Devil or his demons who possess man to do such great evil."

Abbot: "Son, of all the sins that emanate from man's ego, the killing of another or even oneself is the worst. Life possesses a great potential that should always be allowed to come to fruition. So, to kill a person is indeed the greatest evil man has ever wrought; and to deny them the opportunity of blossoming to fruition."

Seeker: "Father, is it only man's ego that causes him to kill? Doesn't a man have an instinct for such violence?"

Abbot: "Yes, son, you are right. Man is part of the animal kingdom and is indeed capable of what all the other animals can do, including viciousness and murder. However, though his body is of the animal, his soul is of the Divine and any man acting from his soul is not capable of his lower animal instincts. You may ask, what makes man degenerate to such a beastly low and I'd answer that it is the ego, son. For that, which is hurt in man, is the ego, and when a man is hurt, his wrath is easily unleashed in manifold forms including murder.

Son, man's egocentric motivation to see another dead may stem from his desperate and ignorant desire for healing and closure from the hurt that was caused to him. It is this venomous desire which is based on the false belief that the death of the offender who caused the hurt would bring to man the closure he so unreasonably seeks that drives vengeance as murder. But son, thus is the man who hasn't tasted the nectar of forgiveness and who is not loving. And thus is the man whose heart hasn't been unburdened and made weightless in the purifying furnace of forgiveness. And thus are the ignorant, vengeful, and murderous seeds sown in mankind, my son. Malady can also descend man from the grace of the Divine to madness and therefore such viciousness. See to it that those afflicted with malady are sequestered and cared for. They may have lost the use of the holy spirit of their minds but their humanity and souls are intact and sacred."

Seeker: "Indeed, father. Please tell me more about the ego and hurt."

Abbot: "Son, the soul cannot be hurt; not by anything conceivable by the human mind. It is the ego and its objects of attachment that is hurt. One man steals the wife of another and the embittered husband kills him, is that not the work of the ego? The husband's ego and its attachment to his wife is hurt and he becomes inconsolably wrathful and seeks revenge. Again, son, one woman covets to be married to a wealthy and famous man and so she plots to kill the man's wife to pave the way for her covetousness. It is the woman's ego that desires the pleasures and comforts of being married to a wealthy and famous man. The father of the murdered wife is inconsolably hurt when he uncovers the plot and seeks revenge. Again, a thief goes into the home of another man to steal his money, and when the homeowner resists, the thief kills him. It is the ego that veils man's love and descends him into brutishness and thievery. Son, do you see that the great evil you speak of is the result of the interplay of egos?"

Seeker: "Yes father, I see."

Abbot: "And when the culprits are brought before the magistrate, he pronounces judgment on them to be executed according to the laws of the country. The magistrate is a functionary of his country's laws and therefore convinces himself that what he is doing is justifiable and lawful. Son, can it be justifiable or lawful to kill human beings under any circumstances?"

Seeker: "No, father, I don't think so. Is the magistrate also acting out his ego?"

Abbot: "Of course, son. When you disrobe the magistrate of his gown, unburden him of his wig, soften his buttocks from his chair, and indeed, unhang him from his ego; what you have left is a simple human being who had been misled by his country's laws and society. Your society gives the magistrate an ego, the lustful man an ego, the jealous man an ego, the covetous woman an ego, the hurt father an ego, the avaricious thief an ego, and then sits back to bemoan the interplay of egos as evil works of the Devil. Ah, the pain of a loveless society my son."

Seeker: "Indeed, father. What about other grievous crimes like mass murders in the name of ethnic cleansing or some other, which have resulted in the deaths of countless millions? Are such perpetrators not possessed by the Devil himself, to take the lives of millions?"

Abbot: "Son, once the insane have been sequestered, the rest are but the miserable actors of their egos. The Devil as I have already told you is a creation of man himself to take the fall for his misdeeds. Son, only egos and maladies can cause a man to act insanely. Man's soul is love and love doesn't hurt; love doesn't know us and them; and love doesn't denigrate any human being, either justifiably, lawfully, or gainfully. Ah, the pain of a loveless society my son."

Seeker: "Father, what about sociopaths or psychopaths who revel in their evil deeds for the sake of causing sorrow and harm to others?"

Abbot: "Son, indeed, there are seemingly sane people among you whose psychologies have become dysfunctional in one way or the other. And as a result, suffer various maladies that your societies have so ably researched and documented. But behind every psychopath or sociopath is a dysfunctional society that turns an innocent child into something they are not. Nobody is born a psychopath or sociopath.

Son, your societies create and enforce laws, norms, conventions, customs, restrictions, expectations and what have you, that may overwhelm an individual's psychology, which is already laden with egocentric tendencies. That is certainly a recipe for disaster and may manifest as antisocial patterns. Only love would make man social, empathetic, and friendly but he cannot love unconditionally without self-knowledge. The ego is always in the way my son."

Seeker: "Indeed, father. What about narcissistic people who slander, backbite, and set people against each other for their amusement or gain?"

Abbot: "Son, narcissism is contained in a person's ego, not their soul. The human soul is love and is incapable of sin. When the soul is veiled by ignorance, the feisty egoistic mind goes to work, doing all its mischievous and wicked deeds. Who, being self-realized and centered in self-knowledge would be mischievous? Self-knowledge reveals to man his equality with the rest of the world and it opens his heart to kindness. His steps and handiwork are guided by intelligence and therefore he is incapable of hurting others. He seeks unity and collective progress; and is a unifying force in his society."

Seeker: "Father, I realize from the foregoing that people must be encouraged to love unconditionally to promote a healthy society. Is that not so?"

Abbot: "Son, encouraging people to love is not the solution to a healthy society. Love is not something people have to choose to do; it is a resultant quality of self-knowledge. The soul naturally is effulgent with love and is only brought to the foreground when the ego is not. If someone loves because of being told to do so, is that love? If someone loves with a motive to be loved back or praised by his fellows, is that love? If the lover seeks to possess the beloved, would it still be loving and not hurt? And can love be exacted? Can faith be exacted? Can respect be exacted? Can happiness be summoned? Then where is it on Earth my son?

If someone loves his family and hates other families, or loves his country and hates other countries, or loves his race and hates other races, does he know the meaning of love?"

Seeker: "Indeed not, father. Could you please tell me about the lover not seeking to possess the beloved?"

Abbot: "Man's nature is love and that which he calls love is a certain strong feeling and yearning he occasionally encounters when certain things trigger it because he is egocentric and not always loving. It's a yearning for wonderment and awe, for Oneness, and for a place where man feels he belongs. There's intensity and elevation of vibration, requiring faster heartbeats and bringing sweetness to man when he is seized by the sudden onrush of energy. That sweetness is what man longs for but son, he makes the mistake of situating or attaching the sweetness in the objects that trigger the feeling and yearning of love; without knowing that the sweetness is in the longing, the yearning, and the capacity to express love. When man comes to a clear self-perceived understanding that the yearning and indeed, the loving is a symphony of Oneness, then he has arrived in the state or quality of his person that loves for the sake of lovingness and not for the myriad objects that elicit the feeling of love. Ah, the plenitude of love my son."

Seeker: "Indeed, father. What are some of the things that trigger the feeling of the sweetness of love?"

Abbot: "Many things, my son; and are all about man everywhere he looks. Beauty is one of the things and harmony is the painter of beauty. The beautiful and harmonious face or physique of a woman or a man brings about the quality of lovingness to the beholder. Charm is one of the things and reciprocity is its rhythm. Melody is one of the things and joy is what she gifts her lover. A beautiful sky, landscape, and indeed, the face of nature may yet ignite the feeling in man my son. When the lover seeks to possess and keep the beloved, he only strives for love and it may elude him. Can man possess the beautiful sky? Can he possess beauty in his pocket and go about with it? Can he possess his fellow to constantly excite his lovingness? If the beloved loves to stay, has the lover not defeated the need to possess the beloved and its hurts? And so, can the beloved, if they are human and not the sight of the Milky Way, become lovers too? Can all men and all women be lovers and let the face of nature and therefore the Divine be the beloved?

Again son, can man be in a state of lovingness and discard the need to be loved by another? For if a man seeks to become beloved and takes satisfaction from being loved by another, he is merely being egotistic and conceited. But if both are lovers, then there's only lovingness which is the goal of relationships."

Seeker: "Indeed, father. What is the relationship between love and hate?"

Abbot: "Son, love by nature is unconditional; meaning it cannot be selective in its giving. A heart that can love and hate at the same time is merely acting out its ego; for where there is love the concept or idea of hate cannot arise. Love and hate can only co-exist as ideas, as opposites. But truth has no opposite because truth is 'what is' and that which is, cannot be contradicted, and does not have an opposite. When you speak of encouraging people to love, you are engaging in idealism; that is, you're speaking of love as an idea, which should be pursued to offset the reality of hate in your society. Therefore, love in this context is the ideal state of the reality of hate in your society, which is due to the interplay of egos. And an ego that loves in reaction to its hate is merely conceited, not loving.

As I have already told you, son, love does not have an opposite and it is not an idea; it is a resultant quality of self-knowledge that emanates from the soul of man. When man is acting from his soul, he drools effortlessly with love, true love, which is not conditioned by some idealism but is the natural state of the man who so authentically lives his life. If man wants a healthy society, he can only get it through self-inquiry, leading him to self-knowledge, which opens the valves for the soul substance of man to come afield through his interface with society. It is only then that love reigns and society is healthy, my son."

Seeker: "Father, is forgiveness related to the quality of love?"

Abbot: "Yes indeed, son. Man may utter some words to say to another that she is forgiven but the veracity of those words depends very much on the authenticity of his love. Son, forgiveness purifies man's love every time he forgives and smiles from the heart and eyes; for the heart goes where the mind cannot go and the eyes never lie. Men have said to one another to forgive but not to forget but we say to man to forgive and forget the forgiveness; for if the forgiveness is remembered so is the hurt, and if the hurt is remembered the forgiveness was not genuine. When the truth of forgiveness dawns on man, the hurt dissolves in the ecstasy that the truth brings to the heart. And therefore, relief of a great burden. Alas, forgive, man, forgive.

Son, only a heart that is centered in love can truly forgive and still love as fervently as before. Ah, the purifying power of forgiveness my son."

Seeker: "Indeed, father. I see from your previous statements that desire plays a huge role in the works of the ego. Like the woman who desires to be married to a wealthy and famous man or the thief who desires the money of another man. Father, what happens between the conception of a desire and the actualization of that which is desired? What moves the limbs of man to actualize something desired, which ought to be known to the desirer as evil, I mean the plotting, the revenge, etc.?"

Abbot: "Great question, son. Desire exists in man because he wants to do as he likes regardless of what he must do or despite what is required of him. This is so because man has free will to choose what role to play and what path to take. And he has free will because his circle is complete and he is therefore of independent mind. So, man has the free will to desire one thing against the other or to choose one thing among many alternatives. Even the choice to hold on to his illusions is still man's own to exercise; and so is the choice to self-inquire.

The compass of the soul is love which always does right because what is right is not a matter of choice but is a matter of course, of clarity, and in one direction. The compass of the ego is the intellect which chooses based on imperfect memories, distorted realities, surrealistic imaginations, fantastic idealisms, and alas, wishes, hopes, and beliefs.

Son, the act of choosing is a result of confusion. He who has clarity in his mind does not choose among possible paths for there is only one path, one direction, and alas, one truth. The woman who desires to be married to a wealthy and famous man chooses between the comforts and pleasures of wealth and fame despite her poor loving husband. She is confused and is directed by the compass of her ego to choose artificial wealth over the natural wealth of love. And her covetousness is fueled by her dysfunctional society which accords respect and prestige to the objects of her desire. If she or the thief were directed by the compass of their souls, she would love and cherish her poor husband and the thief would labor for his bread. For both she and the thief are the same; they covet something that is not theirs. Ah, the missing compass of the soul my son."

Seeker: "Indeed, father. But what moves them to actualize their plots knowing it is evil?"

Abbot: "Son, man is a very capable creature with a very clever intellect. The action or the will of a desire is the easy part. The choice or decision to do is also the action of doing; for man does righteous or sinful deeds from his heart and mind long before he kicks them into action. The physical action of executing a decision is the expression of the choice in time and once the clock starts ticking, it ticks. And there are no second-guesses unless the desire and therefore the will is not strong enough. The intellect can invent plots as quickly as mercury; and can execute its plots just as quickly if the desire is strong. Son, they say, where there is a will, there is a way. Ah, the feistiness of the intellect my son."

Seeker: "Indeed. Father, you said choosing implies confusion, but men have been known to move from one religion to the other, one idea to the other, one persuasion to the other; back and forth. Is man confused?"

Abbot: "Son, if you were presented with two bottles and the first bottle was labeled 'poison, death' and the second labeled 'medicine, health'; would the decision to drink from the second bottle be a choice or evidence of your sanity? And would your decision to drink from the second bottle be instantaneous or would you have to contemplate first?"

Seeker: "Father, it'd be evidence of my sanity and of course, my decision would be instantaneous."

Abbot: "Correct, son. What is right and true does not come from a place of confusion and does not require thinking or analyzing; for the process of thinking, analyzing, comparing, evaluating, and choosing is occasioned by uncertainty, by confusion. Perception is instantaneous."

Seeker: "Indeed, father."

Abbot: "Again son, you suddenly find yourself in a place where you're told that you and everyone else are condemned prisoners, guilty of a grand crime. There are two barrels from which condemned prisoners in a queue must drink some liquids. The first barrel is labeled 'poison, die quickly and painfully' and the second is labeled 'poison, watch body rot and die slowly' and there's a note that says choose one. After an hour, you have watched as all those before you in the queue took cups from prison guards and fetched from either barrel, drank, and went through a door behind the barrels which was marked 'guilty', never to be seen or to be heard of again. It is now your turn; from which barrel would you drink?"

Seeker: "Father, I would find both choices objectionable. And I'd probably not be convinced that I am guilty and should die."

Abbot: "But you have watched as all those before you obsequiously drank from either barrel."

Seeker: "I cannot speak for others, father. I would want to enquire for clarity before I commit myself to any decision or action."

Abbot: "Son, the decision is also the action. When you inquired from the prison guards why you've been imprisoned, they beat you up and called you names. When you asked whether you could appeal to the judge, they beat you up some more and told you that the judge could not be reached and did not speak directly to prisoners. They insisted you must drink from either barrel and handed you a cup. What would you do then?"

Seeker: "Father, it does not seem fair or right to me that I should die of a crime I know nothing of, much less by suicide. I would still insist on knowing more."

Abbot: "Then they beat you up some more, spat on you, and called you even more names. Finally, they carried you from the floor, sent you back in line, and asked you to contemplate and reach a decision before it was your turn again. This was repeated a few times and now you could feel the life in you withering from exhaustion and your resolve began to cave in as more and more prisoners conformed and drank from either barrel. What would you now make of your situation?"

Seeker: "What a conundrum, father."

Abbot: "But you might be tempted to conform too, wouldn't you?"

Seeker: "I guess."

Abbot: "If you had conformed like the rest had and made a choice, then that decision would be uninformed and borne of confusion, fear, and acceptance of guilt of a crime you know nothing of. Is that not so?"

Seeker: "Father, it is so."

Abbot: "But the more you self-inquired, the more certain you became that you were not guilty. A certitude that was borne of your very being and soul; the refutation of which would betray the very thing you have come to know as you. Armed with this faith in truth, you looked around the prison, in your determination and despite the veil of mist and dust, you saw another door far from the one behind the poisonous barrels. This other door had no barrel, no prison guards and there was a label on the door that said 'not guilty'. What would you do then?"

Seeker: "I would be relieved and would immediately abandon the conundrum of the two poisonous barrels, and elect to go through the second door."

Abbot: "Even though you do not know what lies beyond the not-guilty door and what would become of you?"

Seeker: "Yes father, I would rely on my conviction and faith in my innocence and would gladly embrace what lies beyond the not-guilty door."

Abbot: "Correct, son. And that decision would be instantaneous and borne of clarity and certainty."

Seeker: "Indeed, father. Is this riddle relatable to mankind?"

Abbot: "It is the very situation a human being finds himself in when he is born on Earth. Religious authorities pronounce man guilty right from the cradle and he is asked to choose a persuasion that poisons his humanity with dogmas and hate against dissenters, his fellows. Son, can man boast of freedom if he has not yet known and held onto his individuality against the pressures of external influences? Not just in words but in deeds, conviction, and in the actuality of his everyday living principles?

And what does it mean for a man to be an individual if not his 'being' without all externalities of his circle? Including the traditions and doctrines of his culture? And his beliefs, his scriptures, his dogmas, and the myriad authorities that produced them? His prophets and oracles? His heroes and villains? His temples and holy sites? His gurus and pastors? Is man sheep to need a shepherd? Do wolves need a shepherd and why not? Aren't wolves the true seekers of truth, for unity and a pack? And aren't sheep led to their slaughter for food after years of fattening? Could they find truth in the stomachs of their shepherds? Alas.

Son, can a man be without all these and be an individual, alone, unafraid, and with faith in self-knowledge and understanding of his world and himself? Can he? Until then, can man boast of liberation and therefore enlightenment? Until he has destroyed all the fetters of his mind and brought it under the command of Spirit, can he?

Can man boast of the highest virtue of knowing and therefore self-knowledge if all he knows and believes is fed to him through the gullible and fearful forces of his ego? Son, can man boast of his knowledge if it is second-hand? Can he, if it lacks the originality with which the Divine could have expressed Itself in the soul of his person? Can he who lacks originality in his thinking and expression have a vote in a matter concerning people who ought to think and express their lives originally?

And is a man's life not nature's search for authenticity and originality through a particular point of view and expression? And if one were to neglect their duty for originality and living authentically, to take shelter in belief and its false sense of security in dogmas and authorities, are they in tandem with nature's dictates and teleology? Ah, the originality of individuality! Ah, man, why have you ceded your originality and individuality to truth-mufflers for mere pieces of silver, why have you betrayed yourselves?

Son, man is whipped away from his innocence into guilt, conformity, and bigotry. He is promised freedom after his death but in the meantime, he should suffer the pain of the poisoning of his soul and the denial of his free will. Ah, the veil of the not-guilty door my son."

Seeker: "Indeed, father. But there are other benefits of religion and congregations for man. For instance, Father, there's so much sorrow in the world and religion is an avenue for inspiration, consolation, and community. What do you make of this considering congregational or social worship?"

Abbot: "To be a man is to be social and man's soul longs for society and relationships. For man can only know man through man and in knowing the other through relationship he knows himself, son. It is good for the soul to associate with like-minded folks as well as self-realized people with common grounds. After all, man cannot live in isolation from the world, the action of love dictates and requires man to act for the upliftment and progress of the world through the community he finds himself in. And if his community is not that which he fits in, then he ought to create and nurture one that is conducive to the soul.

Indeed, son, sorrow has taken a hefty toll on man for far too long. It deprives him of joy and suffocates his soul, his love. Sorrow comes, but man hangs on to it like a Kangaroo to its baby. He hugs sorrow so affectionately and breastfeeds it, day, and night. Even when asleep, he still holds on to his sorrow and dreams about it; clouding Morpheus and our door. Man receives sorrow like a seed and plants it in fertile soil, with bitter excitement; he waters it in the morning, clears the surrounding weeds in the afternoon, waters it again in the evening, and during the night, he hums melodies to the infant plant. Son, man cultivates sorrow and only he, himself, can de-cultivate it.

You said a man needs consolation and inspiration when sorrowful and so he joins a religion? Does he? The soul of man does not need pity or words of encouragement; pity is for the dead and words have no meaning for the soul. That which is sorrowful in man is not his soul for that is impossible; it is the ego and its attachments. When the ego is separated from any of its attachments; there is sorrow, or there is anger, or there is despair, or there is depression and alas, there is pain. All of these are works of the ego; the false self that man has become so fond of despite his nature.

Man is aggrieved and gripped by sorrow when death comes to take his parent, child, or loved one. But he is indifferent, happy, and celebrates when death comes for his enemy or someone he hates. Is that not the hypocrisy of the false self?"

Seeker: "Father, is it hypocrisy to mourn the death of one's parent or child and be happy about the death of a known thief?"

Abbot: "Son, mourn for your loved ones and mourn for the transitioning of all souls. Mourning is the celebration of life itself and ought to remind man of the value of his life. Mourning brings man closer to death and ought to remind him of the shortness of his life. All deaths are mournful and all lives are potentials, son. The whole world ought to mourn for the death of a parent or a child, no matter whose parent or child they were. In the aged parent is the loss of his love which he shared with the world and in the infant child is the loss of all the marvelous potentials that could benefit the world. Both are losses and the whole world ought to mourn for them. Similarly, in a thief also, are the loss of all the marvelous potentials a reformed thief could possess and help his world.

Son, it is indeed a hypocrisy to mourn for the death of a loved one and celebrate for the death of others; just as it is to love oneself and hate others. And remember, where there's love, true love, the idea of hate cannot raise its ugly head. You are all souls and that which is added to you by your society is a mere garment; wear it modestly. Where your neighbor's garment is dirty, offer them soap and water, for they might return the favor in later years. Ah, the missing compass of the soul my son."

Seeker: "Indeed, father. Please tell me more about man and sorrow."

Abbot: "Son, sorrow results from many things. When one feels guilty of a sin or something awful, they become sorrowful. When one loses a loved one, they become sorrowful. When one is angry or in despair for not achieving an ambition or a desire, one becomes sorrowful. When one loves another and is not loved back, they become sorrowful. Sorrow is what happens after a cherished thing is lost, or before a desired thing is gained. The absence of the thing and its associated pleasures causes man to be sorrowful; which disturbs his inner tranquility and joy.

The loss of one's innocence and its associated freedom from guilt, and the loss of a loved one and the associated pleasures of their memories, the comforts, and companionship they shared, can overwhelm a man with sorrow. Also, the frustration of not achieving a status or the agony of an unreciprocated love and their associated pleasures can equally ignite sorrow in man.

Son, to brood over that which causes sorrow, only sustains, and prolongs sorrow. As I have already told you, many things cause sorrow, and wisdom is to not brood over them. Death comes but life goes on and pain comes but love is stronger. The mind that broods over sorrow is not wholistic and therefore does not possess the full vigor of the holy spirit of mind. Alas, it is the egoistic mind."

Seeker: "Is it the mind that prolongs sorrow?"

Abbot: "Yes indeed. It is the egoistic mind, son, that prolongs the feeling of sorrow and calls it pain, and it is the self-same egoistic mind that prolongs the feeling of pleasure and calls it happy. That which it calls pain makes man violent, hateful, envious, jealous, and alas, egocentric. And that which it calls happy also makes man violent, hateful, envious, jealous, and alas, egocentric. If man were wiser than he pretends to be, then surely, his mind would be one and wholistic. Ah, the missing compass of the soul my son."

Seeker: "Indeed, father. What about life's challenges that man faces at every turn?"

Abbot: "Son, man faces two sets of challenges; necessary ones and unnecessary ones. The necessary ones are few but the unnecessary ones are manifold. Man faces the challenges of his bodily needs, which are necessary and he faces the challenges of his psychological desires, which are unnecessary. Healthy food and clean water are necessary for the body and so are the safety of a reasonable shelter and the warmth of clothing. His heart also longs for community and relationships but is repulsed and challenged by his dysfunctional society.

Man is given a personality by his society and that false self or the ego, has needs. Because the ego compares and competes, man is faced with the challenge of one-upmanship, from the classroom to the boardroom. Because man's society worships wealth and because the ego covets it, he is faced with the challenge of amassing wealth. Because the rich and famous are celebrated and the poor are vilified, the ego strives to distance itself from poverty and this is also a source of challenge for man. Because his ego loves in reaction to its hate or for a motive, his love is unreciprocated and he is challenged.

Because man's ego evaluates and makes judgments of others, it is prone to the injury of the judgment of others and he is hurt, which is also a challenge. Because the feisty ego chases after its objects of attachment, man is ceaselessly occupied with myriad challenges. And because others are also ceaselessly occupied with their challenges, man's society is a clash of selfish and greedy people, haunted by their innumerable unnecessary challenges and tearing each other apart.

Son, only self-realized people can build a world without challenges. Through cooperation and unity, self-realized people would lighten the burdens of one another and through love, poverty could evaporate into thin air in just one generation. Self-knowledge would quash his selfishness and greed and would retire his feisty ego from the foreground. But alas, he is not self-realized and does not love, not truly. Ah, the missing compass of the soul my son."

Seeker: "Father, what about congregational worship and giving thanks or praises to God?"

Abbot: "Why do you pour out sweetened words to God? Why do you prostrate to God? Is man hoping to stoke God's vanity and ask for favors? Why do you give praise and thanks to God? Why do you bring your crops and livestock to the altar of God, only to watch them decompose? Is man so conceited as to wish to reward God? Son, remember that man's projection of the Divine as a person is limited and erroneous, and it is out of that limitation and error that he does all these things; deceiving himself that he does his duty. The Divine is all about man and if he wishes to prostrate and give thanks to it, he ought to start with the ants and worms that fertilize your soils; with the bees that pollinate your crops and plants; with the air that fills your lungs and cells; with the crops and livestock that provide you with nourishment; with the birds that delight your ears; with the Sun and all the planets and other cosmic bodies; and alas, with himself. Son, man's only duty is love and he doesn't need a religion for that; he only needs devotion, an expression of love and it is deepest and truest when he resides in the silence and solemnity of his inner sanctuary. Do you suppose that the Divine needed worship and that is why He created man to prostrate to it, serve it, sing its praises, thank it for being a 'good' God, and play this kind of game? And in return, the Divine would do its duty of sustaining Creation? A quid pro quo?"

Seeker: "Indeed not, father. What is the nature of worship?"

Abbot: "Son, worship is a movement away from Oneness to duality, to separation and conflict. Some part of Oneness cannot dominate nor require prostration from some other part of

Oneness; for it is all One, what you worship is you, and what you praise is the self-same you. Isn't it bizarre for the son to worship the father, or even perhaps a sacrilege? Are the father and son not One? Does it do you good to salute yourself in the mirror? Does it?

Son, the intellect leads man away from Oneness into its endless and yield-less groping for dominance, for servitude, and a master; who would tell him what to do and what not to do. Does man wonder that he is his own master? That his free will is his own to exercise? That his faith in the Divine must not be exacted by the Divine? That he ought to surrender his very life to the Almighty Divine? Is man blind inwardly? Ah, how shall the blind see my son?

What is, just is. There's no need to bow to a spade when you call a spade a spade for truth is what it is, and doesn't need nor require man's acquiescence to be. There's no need to bow to the Sun when you call it life-giver for the Sun is no respecter of worship and shines anyway. There's no need to bow to air when you call it breath for in what direction would you face? And there's equally no need to worship rivers and lakes because they provide you with sustenance for that is their nature; to provide sustenance to living things. Son, everything is part and parcel of Oneness; seek no separation.

Man's love for life, truth, and love should endear him in the Divine for many reasons; even for the simple fact of his existence and because it is his ground of being. This is possible only in deep devotion and meditation on the nature of his being and why he has been given this experience called human life in the first place; for what lies beyond death is not known to him yet and cannot be known to him until he goes through the holy gate of death.

Also, worshiping diminishes that which is worshiped. Who is man that his prostration or gifts should mean anything to the Divine?

And why would the Divine have the need to be prostrated to or worshiped? The one God or the Great Circle does its duty with or without man's worship and unsolicited obsequiousness. Son, seek that which is pure and true. Reside in silence and devotion, and let your heart beam and spread the light of love to all and sundry. And if by worship he means devotion and meditation then by all means he is welcome to say so as words have varied potential meanings, my son.

And when he bows down in worship as a follower of some sect, even with its words, rituals, dogmas, mythologies, and promises, man ought to know he does so in reverence of the Divine and his Oneness with the rest of mankind, with its variety of worship and names of the one God. He ought to know this for sure by himself and avoid the noise of confusion and argument over what is true and should be obvious to him. And when he has asked himself and knowing how great he is, would he still follow his old ways?

Again son, the truest form of worship in the sense of showing deference to the Divine is to reside in the silence of one's being to know it and uncover his Oneness with it, rather than wasting words and accolades to it for the Sun rises, fish multiply, birds spread seeds and what he calls Heaven awaits him whether he bows to East, West, North, South or not. Ah, the joy of Heaven. Ah, Eternity! Rejoice for this is the Good News my son, rejoice!

And because of this, man mustn't hanker nor pleasure himself with his numerous intellectual comforts in theology and ideology but rather, know why he must submit; with complete surrender and faith to the Way of the Divine, of Nature. The Way is man's original perception of Truth from his point of view and abiding by her principles, in alignment with the Great Course of Nature, of the Divine. Ah, the power of free will my son."

Seeker: "Indeed, father."

Abbot: "Do you want to hear a parable?"

Seeker: "Of course!"

Abbot: "There was a king whose kingdom was so vast; it had no end. All the people in his kingdom were his sons. There was everything a person could want in this kingdom but there was one place in the kingdom every one of his sons wanted so eagerly to visit, it was called Disco Town. Those who had visited Disco Town before heralded and proclaimed it as a must-see party and everyone wished to go there. They only speculated scanty stories about the party for they had forgotten much of what it was like while they were there, but still spoke of it with deep fondness and wished to go back.

But the opportunity to travel to Disco Town was not given easily. Only the king sanctioned it and any one of his sons who wanted to go there would have had to procure their father's consent and clearance. On one occasion, a group of the king's sons went to him and managed to convince him of his approval and they were all given the invitation to Disco Town. The king inscribed on each of their foreheads the designation, 'Guest of Honor' and so, with great excitement, they jumped into their vehicles to travel to the famed Disco Town.

They drove for many days and nights through the vast kingdom and finally, made a turn to join another road with a sign that said 'Few miles to Disco Town'. They were relieved and sped their cars so fast one after the other on the road to Disco Town, which was bordered on each side by deserts. For many more days and nights, they drove amidst heavy winds and flying desert sands, the only scenery to keep them company was vast deserts, sky-scraping dunes, and giant cactuses.

Lo and behold, they arrived at the entrance of Disco Town, a road sign said 'Welcome to Disco Town, slow down'. There was a three-mile-long traffic at the entrance of a lone tunnel that all cars must go through to enter Disco Town. After the long wait, they entered the nine-mile-long tunnel. But this was no ordinary tunnel, it was filled with blinding bright reddish light. By the time they went out of the tunnel into Disco Town, they were none the wiser as to what had happened in the tunnel. The group that had left their father's kingdom together and had expressed excitement about traveling together was now ungrouped and estranged from one another. Worse is that they had also forgotten everything about who they were and where they had come from. They had forgotten all about their father's kingdom and appeared disoriented.

The nine-mile-long tunnel had erased the memory of each of them to tabula rasa and had also changed their bodies. Where they had driven their cars into, they came out of it on foot and unknown to themselves nor each other."

Seeker: "Father, the parable is interesting. If their bodies were changed, what happened to the designations that were inscribed on their foreheads?"

Abbot: "Erased and forgotten. The Guests of Honor became nobodies upon their arrival. They were each ushered into life in Disco Town by a pair of Disco Towners who took it upon themselves to help them get new designations. The ushers varied in their designations and vocations. Some were poor and others were rich. Some were rulers and others were peasants. Some dwelled in big houses and others were nomadic. Some lived in urban areas and others lived in cottages. Some were soldiers and others were peacekeepers. Some were caterers and others were brewers. Some were entertainers and others were preachers. Some were farmers and others were fishers. Some were servants and others were cleaners. Some were officials and others were laborers. Some were scholars and others were unlettered. Some belonged to religions and others were free. Some were magistrates and others were criminals. And yet still, some were heroes and others were villains.

And so, the new arrivals were distributed to many varied ushers who oriented them into Disco Town and named them after themselves. While most of them had followed in the footsteps of their ushers and namesakes, others pursued their separate paths. After several years, they had become full-fledged Disco Towners who enjoyed or suffered their stations depending on who they became. They produced crops, and livestock and caught fish for the party, that was all about them. They made good music and danced to it and loved other entertainments such as plays and comedies. They cooked good food and made great wines. While some were served and treated with honor, others scrapped leftovers from the kitchens. They also became law-abiding citizens and those of them who faulted the law were imprisoned. The rich and powerful looked down on the poor. And those who had joined religions castigated their peers who had not.

They also learned other customs and ways of Disco Town. They learned lying was good if it served a purpose. They learned thieving was good if you don't get caught. They learned to hate and to be envious and jealous. They learned to be greedy and ambitious for material wealth and fame. They learned to use deception to confuse, control, and frighten their peers to rule over them. They learned how to kill others and how to do all manner of evil. And alas, they only loved occasionally when it suited them.

Those who became poor were embittered and indignant about such an awful place called Disco Town. They would cry and sing sorrowful songs bemoaning and cursing the maker of Disco Town as a clown to have made such a miserable place called Disco Town. It wasn't only the poor who suffered, the rich and powerful also suffered a great deal. For Disco Town was far from perfect, sometimes natural disasters sprung up from nowhere and killed thousands at once, and the people wailed and cursed its maker. Sometimes death came too soon to loved ones and the people wailed and cursed its maker. But the party went on every day, every hour, and every minute.

There was another tunnel at the end of Disco Town Road which was the exit. It was also not ordinary and the one-mile-long tunnel was filled with blinding bright white light. The distance between the two tunnels or the distance of Disco Town Road was relative to each traveler. It was shorter if a traveler left Disco Town young and it was longer for those who left in their old age. But everyone who left went through the lone exit tunnel, which had a road sign that said 'Bon voyage, thank you for visiting Disco Town. We hope to see you back again'.

A few of those who had journeyed together from their father's kingdom were leaving Disco Town together on one occasion and had to go through the exit tunnel. This time around they were privy to the workings of the exit tunnel. When they drove into the one-mile-long tunnel, everything was revealed to them as they were absorbed by the blinding bright white light. Their memories before Disco Town were restored to them at the same time as the loss of their memories of Disco Town but for a brief one-mile-long trip, they could see their two lives juxtaposed before their very eyes.

They laughed that they had lived all their lives in Disco Town bemoaning and cursing its maker, and had also forgotten that they and everyone else were the 'Guests of Honor', sent by their loving father. They also laughed at all the things they had suffered in Disco Town, like wealth for they had not known avarice; like poverty for they had not known measurement; and like death for they had not known dying. And they called it a plaything, a party.

And they wept with sorry and regret that they didn't love more, that they didn't share more, and that they didn't help one another more. They also wept that they had lied and cheated, that they had killed and oppressed their fellow Guests of Honor, and that they didn't make Disco Town a better place. And they called it a lesson, a school ground."

Seeker: "Father, what an exhilarating and curious parable. What is the import of it?"

Abbot: "Son, do not strain for understanding; reside in silence and let it come to you."

Seeker: "Indeed, father."

Abbot: "Son, for most human beings on Earth, self-realization would happen to them while passing through the holy gate of death but that does not help the world. A man ought to seek self-knowledge to find his identity and bring the pristine perfection of the Divine into his imperfect world. Like the two sides of a spectrum; the world of the Divine and the world of creation must draw towards intersection, to perfect Oneness. Man destroys the perfection of Oneness when he alienates himself from it, for he, is the epitome of the world of creation, blessed with the higher senses of the holy spirit of mind and the love of his heart. Only man can bridge the dichotomy which diminishes the luster of life. This is the task at hand and this is what would make man's society healthy."

Seeker: "Indeed, father, I now understand. But father, if a man finds himself on Earth and has no inkling of his origin, shouldn't he just make do and enjoy his life without all the seriousness of self-inquiry and truth? After all, what is the import and example of one life going to do to the collective destiny of man?"

Abbot: "Son, it is this indifference that makes man complacent and ignorant. It is like suddenly finding yourself at a party and all you do is eat, drink, wipe your mouth, and leave the party without asking or knowing whose or what party it was. And when you're asked why, you chuckle and ask, 'What does it matter?', And that you only cared about the food and drinks. This is the sort of folly that makes fools out of people who ought to be wise, son. If a man finds himself on Earth and is blessed with all these gifts he has; shouldn't how a man lives on Earth be extremely important to him more than the pleasures of comforts and the complacency of being carefree? And can man drift to inequity simply on account of his limited perception of where he comes from? Is man blind to his surroundings? Is a man not centered on self-knowledge? Why does he ask to know about his origin? When he has asked himself and knowing how great he is; would he drift to inequity and shoddiness? And when he has asked himself and knowing how great he is; would he shirk his duty to the collective destiny of man?"

Seeker: "Indeed not, father. So, man has a duty foremostly to himself, to know what he is, and, he has a duty to the rest of mankind through cooperation and making the world a better place. What about his duty to his maker?"

Abbot: "Son, in doing his duty to himself; he does his duty to his society. And in doing his duty to his society; man does his duty to his maker. It is all Oneness. Day is not holier than night; neither is night holier than day. What is far could be nearer and what is near could be farther. What is here could be there and what is there could be here. In understanding Oneness, man understands himself, and all-duty becomes clear."

Seeker: "Indeed, father."

Abbot: "Son, do you want to hear a story about truth?"

Seeker: "Of course!"

Abbot: "Son, from our blissful repose, we have indeed witnessed many epochs and innumerable generations of mankind. There were epochs when the nemesis of truth had not yet arisen and people were not confronted with dilemmas and confusions about what is true.

In the earliest of times when the Earth was home to only a few people, for the first Adam was still among you; men lived together on a wide glade surrounded by all the species of flora and fauna. And mankind was as it had been intended by Existence; free and loving, cooperative and unifying.

In that time, the truth was like the most beautiful maiden there ever was and she ran naked, free, and wild among men and their sons. Through the plush gardens and orchards that were rife in the woods surrounding the glade and, in their homes and streets, the truth playfully ran around with the children of man after her as she giggled and teased them and she was teased back amidst joy. Everybody knew the truth for she was naked and not shy; she bore many fruits as men became successful abiding in her warm embrace. Indeed, son, life was as it had been intended by Existence; a Rumba with truth.

There was no scarcity because greed had not yet arisen. There was no selfishness because people shared and lived from their souls. There were no families and tribes because every human being was like a brother unto his fellow and favoritism had not yet arisen. There were no laws and governments because everyone knew what to do and what not to do had not yet arisen. There were no morals because immorality had not yet arisen. There were no priests because mediumship and charlatans had not yet arisen. There were no gods because the one God was obvious to everyone and it needn't be worshipped. There were no kings because aristocracy had not yet been invented. There were no wars because weapons had not yet been devised. There were no soldiers because Generals had not yet reared their ugly heads and megalomania had been known for what it is. There was no enmity among men because there was no division among them.

Many sons were begotten by man and his society became plentiful and outrun the beautiful glade. So, the younger generations veered off into nearby glades and valleys to multiply in their kind and lot, while others went off to far-off countries and became nations of their own. Are you interested in this story, son?"

Seeker: "Father, something tells me all our previous conversations have led us to this story. Please tell me all about it."

Abbot: "Indeed, son. Four great rivers ran through the forests of the glade and headed out to faraway lands that had not yet been trodden by man. The sons of men who left to settle outside the glade were already homesick, for they didn't want to leave. They therefore agreed that the four great rivers would be their umbilical cords to their home in the glade for they surmised that no matter how far away they went, the four great rivers would always guide them back home, to their gardens and orchards. They also loved truth; their maiden whom they had fondly called Sophia. But alas, she could not go in four directions all at once and how could she leave her glade?"

Seeker: "Father, what did they do then?"

Abbot: "The elders of the glade met and discussed among themselves as to how to share Sophia and to carry on with their Rumba. Those sons of men who traveled along the banks of the first great river towards the northeast of the glade took with them the left arm and hand of Sophia and went with it. Those who traveled along the banks of the second great river towards the northwest of the glade took with them the right arm and hand of Sophia. Some of the sons of man traveled southwards, along the banks of the third great river, they went towards the southeast of the glade and took with them the left leg and foot of Sophia and those who went along the banks of the fourth great river took with them the right leg and foot, and traveled southwest. What remained of Sophia still lingered among the gardens and orchards of the glade, playing, and teasing with the children of man who remained on the glade."

Seeker: "Father, so they all went away with a piece of truth?"

Abbot: "Correct, son, that's what happened in that earliest time when the nemesis of truth had not yet arisen."

Seeker: "So what happened afterward?"

Abbot: "Indeed, son, many things happened in the ensuing years. Decades became centuries and the Earth was heavily populated with the sons of man. Mankind also increased its knowledge of the Earth and its environment. They devised many implements and tools to make life easier and learned better ways to till their lands. They diverted rivers into their towns and homes. They became clever artisans and craftsmen, adept at various skills. Their languages trickled down from the glade into many dialects and their cuisines also became varied and plentiful. They still lived peaceably amongst themselves and maintained their cordiality with the glade from whence they had scattered across the Earth.

Their griots created many poems and songs to honor their heritage and commons.

They also created and held a yearly festival which was celebrated by all and sundry for many days on end. The grand celebration of the festival was held on the ninth day of the last month of the year and was duly held on the glade, their ancestral homeland. Emissaries and celebrants would come from all four directions; from North East, North West, South East, and South West towards the glade to celebrate the grand durbar. They would each bring their piece of Sophia and attach it to her main body and the whole truth was heralded and celebrated. After the festival, they would then travel back to their hinterlands, along the banks of the four great rivers, carrying with them their pieces of truth and with contentment and joy."

Seeker: "Father, that sounds like a great arrangement."

Abbot: "Indeed, son, it was. They went on and on for many more centuries and their differences became more pronounced. Those who lived in sunbaked areas became darker in complexion and those who lived in cold weather lost their melanin. They also developed markedly different appetites for food and music. Their languages also arrayed so much from each other that during the grand durbar of their festival, only a few old people understood each other in the old mother tongue. But they still traveled back and forth between the four great rivers and the glade, maintaining their roots, and celebrating their heritage and commons.

Then a winter like no other was visited on Earth. It rained and rained for months and nobody dared to venture out. The four great rivers were filled and they overflowed their banks near the glade; the flood waters swept everything into the ocean. The entire glade and its people had been lost and the area was now buried under thick salt water. The four great rivers had meandered into different shapes and directions, and the Earth was no longer the same afterward.

The sons of man and their descendants who lived far away from the glade had lost their homeland and all sense of direction to it. As the Earth dried up and sunshine became regular, they picked themselves up and went about their lives again. They each held on to their piece of truth and accustomed themselves to it. Many more generations passed and the long winter and her brutalities were forgotten.

There were no more yearly festivals and Sophia was no more remembered as the beautiful maiden she was. Some pieces of her had been scattered among men and other pieces buried under the ocean. Centuries became millennia and men were further separated from each other, cooperation and unity had been lost and gradually every society became more and more entrenched in their piece of truth; upon which they had established the first religions, out of the fear of another disastrous winter. And still, those first religions were also lost to history and newer generations had to invent more and more. Each holding on to a tiny fraction of Sophia as the whole and complete truth."

Seeker: "Father, is Sophia lost forever?"

Abbot: "Son, Sophia is a symbol of truth in this story and as you know, truth cannot die. Truth cannot be dismembered and scattered or buried under the Ocean. This story is about how man became convinced that truth had been lost together with the glade and started to follow others who claimed to have it or know how to get it."

Seeker: "Is that not so?"

Abbot: "Truth is not what had been or what will be. Truth is 'what is' and that which is, is always alive, here, and now, dancing and beckoning its perceiver, its consort, to a Rumba.

Truth cannot be captured by language and put into words. Truth cannot be told by another because the act of speaking is based on words. Truth lives in perception and only he whose perception is pure may discern her. Son, truth is not some arcane knowledge hidden away in some caves or held by privileged men or curated by some great libraries for it is not contained in information. It must be perceived firsthand by oneself. Truth is not to be sought after or strained for; it presents itself in its moment and man must be there at the right time and place to perceive it. Ah, the liveliness of truth my son."

Seeker: "Indeed, father. Please tell me more about truth not being what had been or will be."

Abbot: "Son, is the water of the Oceans the same one that filled the craters and depths of the Oceans ten thousand years ago? And do you imagine that the water will change ten thousand years from now?"

Seeker: "Father, it must be the same water; ten thousand years ago, and from now."

Abbot: "Again, is the sunlight that enters Earth's sphere the same one that photosynthesized the plants ten thousand years ago? And do you imagine that the Sun will change its light ten thousand years from now?"

Seeker: "Never! It must have been the same radiation and will be the same ten thousand years from now."

Abbot: "What about the air that fills your lungs and keeps you alive?"

Seeker: "Father, it must be the same air."

Abbot: "And are the senses of smelling, seeing, hearing, tasting, and feeling worse off or better off ten thousand years ago than they are today?"

Seeker: "Father, no. They must have been the same as they are today. Frankincense must have smelled the same as it does today, the sight of the beauty and majesty of Everest must have been the same as it appears today, crows must have cawed the same way as they do today, salt must have tasted the same as it does today and indeed, the soothing breezes of a beach must equally have felt the same way as it does today. And father, I don't think they will change ten thousand years from now."

Abbot: "Correct, son, truth is always the same; ten thousand years ago, as well as from now."

Seeker: "Indeed, father."

Abbot: "And son, do you think a written description or spoken words preserved through songs in memory can take the place of the actual perception of that which it describes or speaks of? Such that, a written description of sunrays or marine life five thousand years ago is more trustworthy than the actual perception of sunrays and marine life today?"

Seeker: "Father, I think it would be daft to come to such a conclusion."

Abbot: "Indeed, son. Again, do you think some writer, five thousand years ago can capture in words the accuracy of the beauty and majesty of Everest, or explain to you the soothing breezes of a beach?"

Seeker: "Indeed not, father. I would prefer to go to Everest and savor her beauty and majesty myself, and certainly, the actual feeling of the soothing breezes of a beach cannot be captured by language to accuracy, I'd prefer taking a walk to the beach myself and letting my soul loose."

Abbot: "Correct, son. What was true ten thousand years ago is also true today and can be directly perceived by oneself. Remember, son, truth lives in perception; let your perception be pure and be guided by the compass of the soul."

Seeker: "Indeed, father. But father, you did not tell me how wickedness, greed, selfishness, immorality, laws, wars, and others came about on Earth after the destruction of the glade."

Abbot: "Son, good of you to remind me. As the years wore on, many more generations of mankind succeeded their forebears and expanded their societies even to greater numbers and distances. The subsequent generations became even more differentiated and alienated from their fellows as did their cultures and their truths. The one God who had been obvious to them and hadn't been worshipped became many worshipful gods.

The descendants of the Northeasterners claimed the truth was a left arm and hand, and conceived all manner of beliefs and sects around that notion. They insisted their truth was the complete and whole truth, and maintained that their ancestry and culture were holy and cursed the claims of others as palpable falsehoods and the works of malevolent spirits. They worshipped seven great gods and twenty minor gods; whom they claimed had created Earth from the ashes of a once bigger planet that was destroyed by the Sun. They also developed the practice of burning a mark on the left shoulder of their newborns and said it was to remind them of what truth was. Truth, they maintained was a left arm and hand, and called all others ignorant.

The children of the Northwesterners cursed them back and called them pagans for they maintained that truth was rather a right

arm and hand, which detested believers of a left arm and hand.
They also built a giant culture and were prideful of their ancestry
which they claimed to have descended directly from the skies. They
nicknamed themselves 'children of the sky' and even identified
some stars as their home. Truth, they maintained was a right arm
and hand, and called all others ignorant.

The Southeasterners on the other hand heralded their left leg and
foot and built a great culture around their belief that their ancestry
had come from the Oceans. And that, a long time ago, they had
lived under the Oceans with God, who then sent them out of
the water onto land to teach the rest of the world literacy and
civilization. They became obsessed with language and symbols and
maintained it was their divine duty to lead the world away from
heathenism into knowledge. Truth, they said was a left leg and foot,
and called all others ignorant.

The Southwesterners had also increased a great deal in their culture
and beliefs. They were a simple people and didn't make grand
claims about their ancestry for they said they had always lived
on their lands. They still sang folk songs that featured gardens
and orchards that seemed to allude to the destroyed glade. They
dismissed claims that God was in the sky or the Oceans but rather
that God was in everything about them including plants and
stones. When it didn't rain and their crops failed, they would sing
and dance on the hard arid ground until their sweats and tears
seemed to wet the ground on the belief that it would soften the
heart of the clouds. During the dance, the right legs and feet of
the dancers were instrumental in the movements and hitting of the
ground. Truth, they also maintained was a right leg and foot, and
called all others ignorant."

Seeker: "Father, this must be the beginning of the divisions of men and their alienation from the one God and one another."

Abbot: "Indeed, son, it is. As the years and the generations of man wore on more and more, the Earth became a hard place. Rainfall was irregular and crop diseases became rampant. The lack of cooperation and unity among men worsened the situation and scarcity became a regular feature of life. Men fought and killed each other over scarce resources, especially food. Societies had to create and enforce laws; governments were also created to maintain law and order. The people who were selected to lead these governments, in time, enshrined themselves as aristocrats and exacted respect from the people.

As more and more respect and status were given to the leaders of governments, it became prestigious to be a leader, and soon, monarchs emerged and established monarchies and dynasties, and sought even bigger wealth and power. Competition for leadership positions also came to stay as a matter of course. Military skills and strength became very instrumental and Generals were handsomely rewarded and knighted. Soldiers sold their services for bread and more desperate people resorted to more desperate means for sustenance.

In these hardships, poor people lost faith in themselves and the Divine. They turned to false gods and supplicated for livelihoods and less pain. They were misled by charlatans who claimed to be mediums for powerful gods and enjoyed the pleasures and prestige of religious leadership. Indeed son, the inception of the grand deception had dawned and mankind was no longer going to be the same afterwards.

The Southeasterners had succeeded in creating literacy and taught it to the rest of the world, and men wrote and wrote and wrote;

on any amenable surface. Laws were written down, beliefs were written down, dos and don'ts were written down, what was moral and immoral were written down, etc. and man was enjoined to follow the written words. And those who followed were rewarded and those who failed to do so were punished. Man was then whipped away from himself into the written word, and was made to believe truth existed in Scripture, in written verses.

Son, if you must know then know this; words have no definite meanings by themselves for they are shells into which a speaker may infuse potential meanings of what is being spoken, and understanding or misunderstanding of the spoken or written word depends on the audience's capacity or incapacity respectively. Some of the potential meanings of words are more obvious than others; for instance, the word 'come' when spoken to someone is more obvious than the word 'God'. For when the word 'God' is spoken to you, son, you might require more information about the speaker before you can fully understand them. Because the speaker may be a Northeasterner, a Northwesterner, a Southeasterner, or a Southwesterner and the truth could be anything.

Son, truth-mufflers who are hard-bent on skewing public perception to their will may do so using words that are programmable as I have told you. Scripture has become important in people's lives because it is invoked in the name of God, and by the invocation of that word, the brain cells go to sleep for most people. Only an inquiring mind may be able to receive words and pass them through the infallible filter of the soul and intelligence, and discern their truly intended meaning and not their obvious meaning for that may be the bait. Ah, the spelling power of words my son."

Seeker: "Father, but it is said that Scripture is the revelation of God, dictated by His prophets and messengers. Is that not so?"

Abbot: "Son, what God reveals, He reveals through the soul and heart of man, and any man who is centered in his soul and looks inwardly would know God's revelation directly for himself. In the mist and dust, and the thick of ignorance, men accorded such titles as prophets and messengers to the few ones among them who had remained centered in their souls and tried to share their love in words. But the crux of the matter is that truth cannot be told to another for each man is already that which can receive the light of truth, the Word of God. Which is not verbal or descriptive but rather comes at its perceiver in wholes; as epiphanies, insights, or intuitions. So, son, you see why written words cannot be trusted as words of God?"

Seeker: "Yes, father, I do. Father, you were telling me about how man was whipped away from himself into the written word."

Abbot: "Indeed, son. All traces of the center, the glade, were now completely obliterated by salt water and the people of the fringes were at each other's throats, confused, angry, hungry, and loveless. They maimed and killed for status, they lied and cheated for breadcrumbs, they worshipped false gods and supplicated for that which was already theirs, and while soulless and without any higher values, they descended into debauchery and gluttony, avarice, and wickedness. The poor began to believe and accept the existence of some evil character who lurked among men and made them wicked-hearted.

They carried on like that for many more centuries; lying and warring. By the fortieth century of the first epoch, it was clear that the first epoch was hopelessly doomed. The wars became more rampant, and added to their plight were bad weather and pestilence that produced even less food and less tranquility. Famines, wars, and natural disasters claimed most lives. Their civilizations and cultures were mortally threatened and a few communities went into seclusion; hiding in small pockets of settlements across the Earth.

The main lands and cultures eventually tumbled. And so, after four thousand years from the first Adam, that epoch came to a miserable end. More than ninety percent of their populations died and the remaining few founded small agrarian villages in safe havens away from the brutalities of empire builders and warlords. Literacy was eventually lost and all their written material was buried under debris and mud. After a few more decades and generations, all that was left of the first epoch were tales and songs; told and sung amidst tears by old people that said of once thriving civilizations which built giant things and wrought wicked deeds."

Seeker: "Giant things and wicked deeds indeed, father. How did the villages fare?"

Abbot: "Son, the simplicity of village life made it possible for man to revert to his naturalness and thus started to build again, little by little, but the nemesis of truth still lurked."

Seeker: "Father, how many epochs have there been?"

Abbot: "Innumerable."

Seeker: "And they always started and ended the same way?"

Abbot: "Always."

Seeker: "Will man ever learn from his past mistakes?"

Abbot: "He only needs to look to his present opportunities, son."

Seeker: "What are his present opportunities, father?"

Abbot: "Self-knowledge, Self-understanding, and Self-love."

Seeker: "Which will lead to the realization of the collective destiny of mankind?"

Abbot: "Correct, son. Now wake up."

The Abbot of Morpheus | First Epoch | By Gerfarer

Don't miss out!

Visit the website below and you can sign up to receive emails whenever Gerfarer publishes a new book. There's no charge and no obligation.

https://books2read.com/r/B-A-RNKLC-LFECF

Connecting independent readers to independent writers.

About the Author

Gerfarer is the pen name of the author. He is a middle-aged male, who lives at the intersection of certain coordinates on the globe. He drinks tea with a few squeezes of lemon and three sugars in the morning and listens to podcasts before going to sleep in the night. He breaks down everything and then helps you to rebuild it back together and encourages you to discern for yourself. Gerfarer offers a fresh line of questioning and answering which would be interesting to curious people who are seeking liberation.

Read more at https://twitter.com/gerfarer.